Spinoza's Philosophy: An Outline

Spinoza's Philosophy: An Outline

Errol E. Harris

Humanities Press
New Jersey ▼ London

First published in 1992 by Humanities Press International, Inc.,
Atlantic Highlands, New Jersey 07716, and
3 Henrietta Street, Covent Garden, London WC2E 8LU

©1992 by Errol E. Harris

Library of Congress Cataloging-in-Publication Data
Harris, Errol E.
Spinoza's philosophy, an outline / Errol E. Harris.
p.   cm.
Includes bibliographical references and index.
ISBN 0-391-03736-6 (cloth). — ISBN 0-391-03737-4 (pbk.)
1. Spinoza, Benedictus de, 1632–1677.   I. Title.
B3998.H275   1992
199'.492—dc20   91–35694
CIP

A catalog record for this book is available from the British Library.

Printed in the United States of America

Contents

Preface

THIS BOOK IS intended to help students beginning their study of Spinoza to understand his philosophy, by outlining in plain language the main ideas and line of reasoning that he adopts and expounds. The author has tried to do this without overburdening the reader with footnotes or distracting the student from the general line of argument by constant learned references, in the hope that by giving a straightforward account of the philosopher's thought sufficient interest will be kindled to induce the reader to explore the texts and to consult more detailed commentaries, of which a number of the most useful and reliable are listed on page 119.

The best way to use the book is to read it through in order to get a general view of Spinoza's system, and then to reread it along with the texts as a help in unravelling difficulties in Spinoza's exposition. The main work to study is, of course, the *Ethics*, but it is advisable to begin with the unfinished *Treatise on the Improvement of the Intellect*, in order to discover how Spinoza devised the method that he uses in the later work and why he thought it desirable. Although the *Ethics* was written after the *Treatise*, the ideas expounded with meticulous care and precise attention to order in the former were already germinating in the latter. In the footnotes to the *Treatise*, and in references in his correspondence, Spinoza indicated that he intended to complete the work. It may be that he did not live long enough to do so (for he died at the age of 45), or it may be that he reached a point in the *Treatise* at which he realized that he should make a fresh start, using the method he had by then discovered. Be that as it may, once the student has mastered the argument and the doctrine of the *Ethics*, it will be time to explore the *Tractatus Theologico-Politicus* and the *Tractatus Politicus*, which is also an unfinished fragment. Students of political philosophy may wish to reverse this order, but, if they do, they should be warned that the political treatises presuppose the ideas developed in the main work and presume a knowledge of them.

Spinoza, a Portuguese Jew, whose immediate forebears fled from the Spanish Inquisition to settle in Amsterdam, is one of the greatest and most profound thinkers that Western civilization has produced. Much of

his thought was far in advance of his time, and, perhaps for that very
reason, it was reviled and rejected by most of his contemporaries, who
condemned it (often without sufficient knowledge) as atheistic and sub-
versive. It was not until more than a century after his death that interest
was revived in his work, mainly by the German thinkers of the Romantic
revival, whose enthusiastic approval was unreserved; and today his appeal, especially in the Netherlands and in Europe, is as strong as it ever
was. Many of his admirers find his philosophy as satisfying intellectually
and as fulfilling spiritually as any religion. But even if the student is not as
convinced as all that of its finality, the close study of his reasoning and his
concepts can hardly fail to be rewarding, not just as an intellectual
exercise, but also as an inspiration and a guide to practical life.

Spinoza led a somewhat reclusive life about which not much is known,
although he did not altogether shun public affairs, and, it is thought, he
was once proposed as the official political philosopher for the government
of Holland. He was a close friend of the Grand Pensionary, Jan de Witt,
and had other friends who were prominent in public life. But his primary
interest was in philosophy and (in his own phrase) "the improvement of
the intellect," while he earned himself a modest living by grinding lenses
for optical instruments. Students interested in his life and historical
background should consult the biographies by Colerus and Lucas, Abra-
ham Wolfson, R. Willis, K. O. Meinsma, Jacob Freudenthal, and A. Wolf
(in the introduction to his translation of the *Short Treatise on God, Man
and Human Well-being*).

E. E. H.
HIGH WRAY

List of
Spinoza's Chief Works

Korte Verhandeling van God, de Mensch, en deszelfs   (KV)
  Welstand
(*Short Treatise on God, Man and Human Well-being*).

Tractatus de Intellectus Emendatione   (TdIE)
(*Treatise on the Improvement of the Intellect*).

Ethica   (E)
(*Ethics*).

Tractatus Theologico-Politicus   (TTP)
(*Theological-Political Treatise*).

Tractatus Politicus   (TP)
(*Political Treatise*).

Epistolae   (Ep)
(*Epistles*) (Correspondence)

Renati Descartes Principiorum philosophiae, more   (PPD)
  geometrico demonstratae
(*Principles of Philosophy of René Descartes,*
  Demonstrated in the Geometrical Method).

Cogitata Metaphysica   (CM)
(*Metaphysical Reflections*).

Recommended Translations

Boyle, A. *The Ethics of Spinoza and de Intellectus Emendatione.* London
  and New York: Everyman Library, 1910.

Elwes, R. H. M. *The Chief Works of Benedict de Spinoza.* 2 vols. New

York: Dover Publications, 1955. Available in cloth from Magnolia, Mass.: Peter Smith Pub., Inc.

Spinoza, Baruch. *The Ethics and Selected Letters*. Translated by S. Shirley and introduced by S. Feldman. Indianapolis and Cambridge: Hackett Publishing Company, 1982.

Wolf, A. *The Correspondence of Spinoza*. London and New York: Lincoln and McVeagh, 1927.

———. *Spinoza's Short Treatise on God, Man and His Well-being*. New York: Russell and Russell, 1963.

1

Introduction: The Current Appeal of Spinoza's Philosophy

IN THESE DAYS philosophy has very little, if any, obvious relation to the conduct of life. Academic philosophers do not consider their professional occupation, any more than do mathematicians, as having any bearing upon the way they act in other matters or upon their nonprofessional concerns. But this is a comparatively recent development. The tradition that came down to us from Socrates had been, until the early decades of this century, one in which philosophy was a way of life, a total belief which a person regarded as a religion, a commitment to ideals which one made some effort to live up to. It is, therefore, perhaps not altogether surprising to find a seventeenth-century philosopher asking himself at the outset of his reflection what ends in life it would be most satisfactory to pursue, concluding that those most commonly followed were unrewarding and futile and that he could himself most profitably devote his life entirely to the search for truth.

Nowadays, even a decision of this kind has been regarded by some writers as largely meaningless, for, since the 1940s, it has become more common for philosophers to ask, with Pilate, "What is truth?" and usually to adopt a relativistic answer: what most people happen to believe at the time; or else, to deny any general meaning whatsoever to the term "truth," and to assert that, while particular propositions can be true or false, there is no such thing as Truth as such. This is only another way of expressing a relativistic creed, making truth relative not only to the period

1

and the social context, but also to the subject matter under investigation.

Relativism, however, is unsatisfactory both as a theory and as a practical creed. As a theory it refutes itself, for it can claim no more credence on its own showing than any other theory. In practice it abandons the individual to unguided and unprincipled choice, each to follow his or her own arbitrary whim or inclination. The inevitable result would be confusion and conflict, which cannot be resolved by any resort to reason (the appeal of which is to an objective truth), but, if at all, only by force. When sheer might prevails, it becomes futile and meaningless to speak of right, and only the interests of the powerful, the dictator, and the tyrant, are served.

It should not surprise us, then, that the prevalence of relativism in modern times has led to a sense of bewilderment and frustration, and has sent the rising generation wandering in pursuit of assurance and satisfaction down strange paths of permissiveness, extravagant orgies, psychedelic distortions of reality, and irrational withdrawal from society. The rejection of every criterion of truth has led to a search for truth in untruth and illusion, leading in practice as well as in theory to self-refutation, disorientation, and ultimate despair.

Benedict de Spinoza, in contrast, believed that all truth was one single and coherent body of knowledge, itself an integral aspect of the one single indivisible complex of reality, which he called Substance-or-Nature-or-God. This he held to be the sole object of ultimate worth, and the only one devotion to which would give one complete satisfaction. That conclusion he reached early in life, as he tells us, "after experience had taught [him] that all things which commonly occur in life are vain and futile." He thereupon subordinated all other interests and pursuits (which he did not abandon immediately) to the contemplative life; and he acted henceforward, so far as is known, in full accordance with his own teachings and beliefs. His philosophy, in fact, was his religion, and it arose out of studies originally religious in character, from a penetrating questioning of ancient and traditional religious beliefs with which he had, even before he was 20 years old, become dissatisfied.

The early experience that led to his disillusionment with worldly pursuits were varied and, to most young men, would have been deeply disconcerting. Difficulties he found with the Orthodox Jewish religion, in which he had been brought up and educated, led him, in his early twenties, to express doubts and to entertain views about human immortality and the authority of the Bible that the leaders of the Synagogue (his boyhood teachers) found heretical. He had already shown interest in, and was giving assiduous attention to, secular learning: classical literature, mathematics and science, and, in particular, the philosophy of Descartes. This interest in Gentile thought and scholarship alarmed the Jewish rabbinate, who considered it wayward and aberrant.

Under his Jewish mentors he had earlier mastered the Old Testament, the learning of the Talmud and of mediaeval Hebrew writers, but now he sought enlightenment elsewhere. His own thinking led him to very different views of God and human nature from those commonly held, not only by the Jews of his home town, Amsterdam, but also by the Calvinists of the Dutch Reformed Church. Being a man of great intellectual integrity and moral sincerity, Spinoza could not make a public show of conformity to religious observances in which he no longer believed, even though there were still some which he respected and some which he continued to fulfil. Nevertheless, the Jewish authorities sought to call him to account, attempting first to buy his outward conformity with a tempting bribe, which he scorned, and finally expelling him from the Synagogue with fearsome and elaborate curses.

Now free to follow his own independent way, Spinoza devoted himself wholly to learned pursuits, except for the trade of lens-grinding, which he had learned earlier and which enabled him to earn a bare sufficiency. It seems that when he was about 17 years old, he and his brother Gabriel had been together in business (perhaps with the object of succeeding their father, who died not long afterwards). Spinoza had also been involved in lawsuits, not only in connection with commercial debtors, but also later with his own step-sister, when she attempted to exclude him from his patrimony on the pretext of his heretical views. Although he won his case, he allowed his step-sister to keep the whole inheritance, except for his late mother's bedstead. Spinoza, therefore, had had experience of commercial and worldly affairs. Moreover, his father had been influential in the Jewish community and had held office in the Synagogue, so the son was aware of the flavor of public honors. His reflection upon this early experience led him to reject the pursuit of wealth and of pleasure, as well as of secular advancement.

Accordingly, in the treatise from which we have already quoted, he tells us that he had discovered all the objects most frequently desired by men to be empty and fruitless. These reduce mainly to three: pleasure, wealth, and social position. The first, he says, excites and distracts the mind to the detriment of every other pursuit, leaving it unsatisfied and despondent; the second is precarious as well as distracting, and is fraught with dangers threatening disaster; the third has all the disadvantages of the second and in addition constrains one to defer to the opinions of others concerning what is good and bad, right and wrong. Such surrender of his own judgement to the views of the mob was, above all, abhorrent to Spinoza. What he sought was an object of love and devotion which, as he himself puts it, "feeds the mind with joy alone and is free from all pain"—and he found that there was only one such: that which is eternal and infinite.

The discovery of this object comes through philosophy and reflection, although, as we shall see later, there is another way for those who are less intellectually gifted. To philosophy and reflection it was, therefore, that Spinoza turned, and henceforth gave his wholehearted and unremitting attention, his sole motive being the pursuit of the highest good, the surest and most complete satisfaction. This, for him, was the purpose of philosophy; and the study of Spinoza's quest has proved an equal source of satisfaction to others.

To some this might appear to be a totally self-centered doctrine, but in Spinoza's hands it proves quite otherwise. The good he seeks can, he finds, only be common to all and is to be attained only in community. The search for it for oneself is equally and concomitantly the pursuit of it for others; for what is most valuable to man, he maintains, is his fellow-men acting reasonably, "as with one mind," and the conditions of rational life are attainable only in a well-ordered society. Enjoyment of the good life cannot be exclusive and can be experienced only in concert with others. It follows that realizing the good for oneself requires that one strives equally, and by the same effort, to realize it for others, through education, exhortation, service, and social order. If love and devotion to an eternal and infinite object gives ultimate satisfaction, and if this proves to be nothing less than the intellectual love of God, it is just as much the love of one's neighbor, which is inseparable from it and is necessarily involved in it.

Everything we know of Spinoza testifies to his consistent effort to live up to this conviction, and if that is to be a saint, perhaps we ought not to deny him that title. But if saintliness consists in asceticism, total renunciation of the world, and mystical rapture, Spinoza was no saint. While he renounced the common aims of the majority, he neither condemned nor wholly despised them. In moderation, and as means to comfortable living, he commended, and himself indulged in, harmless pleasures (so far as they were available to him). "I enjoy life," he wrote to Willem van Blyenbergh, "and try to live it, not in sorrow and sighing, but in peace, joy and cheerfulness." And in the *Ethics* he writes:

> It is the part of a wise man, I say, both to refresh and to recreate himself in moderation with sweet food and drink as also with scents and the amenity of green plants, with adornments, music, the exertion of games, theatre, and with other recreations of this sort such as anyone can do without any injury to others. (*Ethics*, IV, xlv, S)

Likewise, he exhorted men to civic duty, and he, himself, undertook a mission to the Prince de Condé when the French invaded the Netherlands, perhaps in the hope of obtaining favorable peace terms. Although later he was accused of spying for the French because he went at the invitation of the Prince, he had gone with the concurrence and apparent encouragement of the authorities at the Hague. In his *Tractatus Theologico-Politicus* he commends those who submitted to persecution and who made sacrifices (even of life itself) for the sake of noble political causes, such as the maintenance of religious freedom. And he did not utterly condemn even wealth, so long as it was not sought as an end in itself but was used only as a means to more important objectives.

Further, Spinoza was no mystic, if mysticism consists in blind faith and the experience of incomprehensible emotional ecstasy. He insisted unfailingly on the rationality of the doctrine that he espoused; he sought to expound it in the most systematic fashion; and he held it to be intellectually enlightening as well as emotionally satisfying. Like Descartes, he equated true and adequate ideas with clear and distinct thinking. The intellectual love of God, which he found to be the highest and most blessed state of mind for humanity, was thinking of this sort, what he classified as knowledge of the third and most adequate kind.

Spinoza was, himself, altogether devoid of mercenary desires. He refused the gift of fl. 2,000 offered him by his friend Simon de Vries, who had also (as he was a bachelor) expressed his intention of leaving his fortune to Spinoza; but Spinoza dissuaded him from doing so, arguing that de Vries had a greater obligation to his own brother, Isaac. When Isaac eventually inherited the estate and was directed by Simon's will to make an annual allowance to Spinoza of fl. 500 Spinoza accepted only fl. 300, despite having little means of his own. Again, in times of adversity and need, the offer of the professorship of philosophy at Heidelberg could not attract Spinoza, who never aspired, so he said, to give public instruction, and who refused to submit even to the mildest restriction upon his freedom of thought and expression, required as a condition of the offer, lest it should "disturb the publicly established religion"

(*Ep*, XLVII). Spinoza ignored the suggestion made by Colonel Stouppe, when Spinoza visited the headquarters of the Prince de Condé, that the philosopher should dedicate a work to Louis XIV (then waging war against Holland) in return for a pension. All such conduct was in keeping with what he taught in the *Ethics*: that a wise man would accept no favors, but would decline them with courtesy so as to avoid giving offense.

At the same time, he did not submit meekly to injustice. He sued at law for his rights when his step-sister sought to deprive him of his inheritance, yet he showed the utmost generosity when he won his case. Similarly, after the murder of Jan de Witt, the Grand Pensionary of Holland (who had settled on Spinoza a pension of fl. 200), when his enemies sought to rescind the provision of this small allowance, instead of disputing the issue Spinoza delivered the document bestowing the dispensation on him into the hands of those who sought to take it from him, so that they were shamed into permitting its continuance.

Mastery of the passions was, according to Spinoza, not the primary aim but the main consequence of human moral adequacy. His doctrine has a superficial resemblance to that of the Stoics, whom he admired, but it is not the same. He believed that human freedom was not, as was commonly held, indeterminacy of choice, but was self-determination, entirely by one's own nature, free from external compulsion. This, for him, was action proper, while determination by extraneous causes was passion, the subjection to which he called bondage.

His own conduct was singularly free of uncontrolled passion. His expulsion from the Synagogue led to no recriminations. He never mentions the event in his writings; in his letters he never complains of injustice at the hands of the Jewish authorities. He seems to have harbored no resentment against his former teachers, nor to have suffered any adverse reaction against the Judaic tradition of learning. His comments give no sign of prejudice, and he retained the deepest respect for Hebrew scholarship and veneration for the Jewish martyrs to persecution. When adverse criticism of his writings (which was plentiful in his lifetime) was stupid, he treated it with contempt, but he seemed never to resent fair comment when it was motivated by sincere scholarship and respect for truth. His correspondence shows the utmost patience and courtesy with disputants who were sometimes obtuse, persistent, and imperceptive.

On the other hand, Spinoza neither believed it possible for human beings to become free of passion, nor did he advocate complete suppression of emotion and desire. As finite beings, he held, we can never wholly free ourselves from the overwhelming forces of external causes, and in times of great stress especially, even the wisest and most steadfast are liable to be overcome. But, apart from inherent human weakness, rational and free action itself was not devoid of emotion—quite the contrary. Such action was, in Spinoza's view, the highest fruit of man's urge to realize his own true essence, the power of the intellect, and it was always accompanied by pleasant and invigorating emotion.

When the de Witt brothers were torn to pieces by the mob, Spinoza broke down in tears. Not only was he overcome by grief but also consumed by anger. He wrote a placard denouncing "the lowest of all barbarians," and would have gone out fearlessly to post it outside the prison where the murder was perpetrated had his landlord not prevented him by locking the door of his lodging. Spinoza lacked neither passion nor courage. When the same mob as had murdered his patron threatened him, accusing him of spying for the French, he offered to go out to meet them and defend his integrity, fearless of the consequences and conscious of his own innocence and patriotic loyalty.

In fine, Spinoza genuinely lived his philosophy as the truly devout live according to their religion. He showed no trace either of hypocrisy or compromise, but practised what he preached, a doctrine of which he was convinced by the most cogent reasoning. For him, indeed, philosophy was a way of life, and what he wrote should be read as such. It is not to be viewed merely as theorizing for its own sake, or as a pure exercise in logic. Certainly, Spinoza adopted the most rigorous form of exposition he could devise, but this was a means to the attainment of what he regarded as unassailable truth; the method was not an end in itself. He believed that his geometrical reasoning established its conclusions, not infallibly (for he had used it to expound the philosophy of Descartes, which in part he believed to be false), but objectively and without special pleading or subjective appeal. So strongly was he convinced of the soundness of his conclusions that when he was challenged by Albert de Burgh, who asked him "How do you know that your philosophy is the best of all those which have ever been taught in the world, are taught even now, or ever will be taught in future?" Spinoza replied: "I do not presume that I have discovered the best philosophy, but I know that I understand the true one. If you ask how I know that, I shall answer, in the same way as you know that the three angles of a triangle are equal to two right angles." Thus, by the geometrical method, he believed that he had established objectively the truth of morality and religion—the true universal religion, as opposed to the superstitions of the vulgar and of the sects.

Would any contemporary thinker allow such a claim?—probably not. Before and since Spinoza's time attempts have been made to establish metaphysics and ethics as exact sciences, but none has succeeded in enlisting widespread support. Spinoza's claim to have set out a scientific demonstration of metaphysical truth is tacit rather than open; but the above quotation makes it clear, along with other passages in his works, that he was sure such demonstration could be given. The belief in objective standards of value and truth implies the possibility of demonstrating their existence, and the theoretical and practical consequences of the alternative are much less attractive.

If relativism holds, value statements and moral demands must be reducible either to expressions of feeling and sentiment or to the ideology of a particular social group. The former alternative completely undermines the notion of moral obligation, for one person's sentiment is as good as another's, and where conflicts occur there can be no obligation to follow one rather than the other. In fact, the same is true even for the single individual. If rational considerations are able to play at best a subsidiary role in decision-making, conflicts between motives can be resolved only by the domination of the stronger emotion; and unless values are based upon some rational foundation, the ultimate determinant of practical choice can only be feeling. In that case, if every statement of value were no more than an expression of feeling, there could be no differentiation between inclination and duty, and thus no basis for any morality.

Social custom might create more appreciable demands, but once they are generally recognized as purely conventional the sense of obligation attached to them dissolves away. Then conformity to the customary rule could be assured only by the imposition of some sort of penalty for violation, whether purely psychological or more violently physical. But moral conduct cannot be maintained merely by the application of sanctions (of whatever kind), because if the fear of penalties is the sole motivation for observance, successful evasion of them would be more attractive than conformity to the rule, mutual trust among mankind could never be warranted, and the maintenance of orderly life would become wholly precarious. This is the moral of Glaucon's argument in the Second Book of Plato's *Republic*, which Socrates, in defense of sound morality, is called upon to refute.

If moral standards are not to be purely relative, however, they must be somehow rooted in the nature of things. Value must be derivable from fact, despite everything that has been maintained (since Hume) in condemnation of the natural fallacy; and standards must be discoverable by investigation of reality through objective methods of inquiry.

Spinoza's doctrine reconciles and validates both sides of this dispute about facts and values. He shows that common criteria of good and evil *are* subjective, and, as generally applied, the terms *are* purely relative in more ways than one. Nevertheless, the very fact that this is so is rooted in the actual nature of human personality as can be objectively demonstrated. By the same token, and deducible from the same factual nature of humanity and of the world of which it is a part, an ideal condition of persons and of society can be revealed, the realization of which would afford all who experienced it peace of mind and satisfaction of spirit. The demand and craving for this satisfaction springs from the intelligent capacity of human beings, which is equally the source of objective knowledge; and the cultivation of both to the utmost possible extent is the key that Spinoza offers to the problem of human existence.

His ethical teaching makes no mention of obligation or of moral imperatives, for he maintains that human wickedness is not a matter of free choice, but is the result of causes external to the "essence" of the delinquent person. To correct the error the causes must be removed and action must be promoted by that essence itself as constituted by the power of reason. Only such action is free, virtuous, and responsible. The law by which it is enjoined is self-imposed and is motivated by the urge within the person (as a "finite mode") to maintain itself in its own essence, its own specific being, to perfect its own nature and increase its own true power of action. Consequently, morality for Spinoza is not submission to any alien rule, but is determination by the law of one's own nature. Yet that again is no arbitrary or capricious whim, but is the expression and realization of the infinite, divine totality which is the immanent cause of all things—a law, therefore, which is universal and objective.

Thus briefly stated, the doctrine may seem to lack demonstrative cogency, even if to many it has intuitive appeal. We shall give a more detailed account of it in succeeding chapters. The appeal, however, is to those who seek practical guidance as well as intellectual satisfaction, but not to those who merely insist upon theoretical meticulousness. If contemporary philosophy has ceased to provide such practical guidance to the ordinary person, it is not simply because it differs from Spinoza's (in some forms) in its technical aridity and abstraction, or (in others) in its impervious obscurity, for Spinoza's writing is by no means free from technicality and obscurity. It is because the positive teaching, or the tacit presupposition, of contemporary thinking misses the profound truth that Spinoza grasped and unremittingly endeavored to render explicit, intelligible, and irrefutibly demonstrable.

Spinoza's method of doing this, however, makes his exposition difficult to follow for the untutored reader, and his use of technical terms that have long since become obsolete makes it hard to understand. An attempt is therefore excusable to present his doctrine in plainer language, as an introduction for the layman and the student unfamiliar with its technicalities, possibly also as an inducement to further reading on the subject. It may be well to begin with a fuller explanation of Spinoza's method, in the hope of mitigating to some extent its appearance of technical asperity.

2

Rationalism and Deductive Method

IN THE HISTORY of modern Western philosophy, Spinoza is usually classed with Descartes and Leibniz as a rationalist, in opposition to the empiricists Thomas Hobbes and John Locke. There is much in the writings and opinions of these philosophers to justify such a grouping, but there is almost as much to warrant quite different associations. Descartes and Locke have many affinities which this classification into opposing schools obscures, and so do Hobbes and Spinoza. But apart from that, while Spinoza is in a significant sense of the word an inveterate rationalist, he is also a great deal more than is commonly understood by that term. While in many respects he was strongly influenced by Descartes and followed his lead, on many important issues he diverged widely from the Cartesian view. The influence upon Spinoza's thought of Maimonides and the mediaeval Jewish writers, as well as the Arabic thinkers against whom their arguments were often pitted, was probably as great as that of Descartes. Also, although he scarcely mentions Plato and Aristotle,* Spinoza's own doctrine, especially in ethics, has important similarities to Plato's, and, as regards his conception of the human soul, to that of Aristotle.

When one speaks of rationalists and empiricists one thinks, as a rule, of the former as people who believe that all knowledge worthy of the name is rationally deduced from self-evident first principles, and of the latter as

---

* There is one reference to "those who follow" these philosophers in the early treatise *On God, Man and Human Well-being* and a somewhat disparaging mention of Plato in the 46th letter.

those who think that only what is derived from sense-perception can rank as reliable knowledge about the world, while the scope of pure reason is severely limited. There are others, however, who maintain that these two positions are but opposite sides of the same coin and that as empirical knowledge involves rational elements so rational deduction depends on experience. While Spinoza's procedure and his explicit teaching give the appearance of rationalism (in the above sense) careful attention to his reasoning will reveal a strong tendency in his thinking to the third variety of philosophy which reconciles the two extremes. The justification of this claim will have to be made as we proceed, first let us note another feature of his work which distinguishes him from Descartes and aligns him more nearly with the ancients.

For Socrates and Plato and, we may say, for most Graeco-Roman writers, philosophy was a way of life and in large measure took the place of religion in modern times. The primary interest of the philosophers was in the question how men ought to live, and their metaphysical and other speculations were undertaken for the sake of the light they could throw on this central consideration. The motivation of Spinoza's philosophy was similar. His interest was predominantly ethical, and even religious, much as he was accused in his own day of atheism and is interpreted by many in our day as a proponent of humanistic naturalism. Descartes, on the other hand, was interested predominantly in logic and the natural sciences, his main concern in philosophy being the validity of knowledge and the best method of acquiring it. Morals and ethics are not prominent in his writings.

Spinoza was clearly aware of the importance of all these matters, but for him they were all ancillary to human salvation. His great work and the one which encompassed his whole system of philosophy is the *Ethics* and the name rightly indicates its ultimate interest. The tone and objective of his philosophy is unmistakably set by the opening of his earlier unfinished *Treatise on the Improvement of the Intellect* where he briefly reviews his attempts in early life to find satisfaction in the common aims of men: pleasure, wealth, and social standing, all of which prove frustrating, and recalls how he decided to devote himself single-mindedly to the pursuit of an objective, not transitory or self-defeating like these, but a true good, which once acquired would give continuous, eternal, and supreme happiness. "All happiness and unhappiness" (he says)

> depend on the quality of the object to which we cleave with love, for strife never arises over that which is not loved, nor will sorrow

be caused if it perishes, nor envy if another possesses it, nor fear, nor hate nor, in a word, any disturbance of the mind; all of which occur in the love of perishable things. . . . But love towards a thing eternal and infinite feeds the mind with joy alone and is free of all pain. That indeed is to be desired and should be sought with all one's strength.

The proof of the existence of such an infinite and eternal object, and the search for understanding and clear conception of it are the central themes of all Spinoza's thinking. He believed that the very nature, or essence, of this object, once grasped, gives its own guarantee of existence, and from it everything else follows of necessity, both adequate knowledge and tranquility of spirit.

As we shall see presently, there can be one and only one infinite and eternal object, and that by its nature it is all-inclusive. This totality is what Spinoza calls Substance, or God, and it is the idea of God that is the foundation of what he distinguishes as the right method of procedure, the most adequate form of knowledge, and the best kind of life. In short, the keynote of his philosophy is unity—the unity of substance, of truth, and of goodness, the explanation of which, in all three aspects, will be the aim of our exposition. Let us begin, as Spinoza did in the *Tractatus de Intellectus Emendatione* with the nature of truth and the "due order" of its discovery.

Spinoza's first published book was an exposition of the philosophy of Descartes "demonstrated in geometrical fashion," and his own chief work, the *Ethics*, is set out entirely "in geometrical order." Descartes, in the reply to the second set of objections to his *Meditations*, had maintained that his arguments could be demonstrated geometrically and gave a specimen of the method. It would follow from the conception of scientific knowledge Descartes espoused that this form of deductive reasoning was the right one, for he believed that one should analyze all problems down to their simplest elements, which would be intuitively intelligible, and then deduce from these, by self-evident steps, the conclusions that were being sought. Such procedure is precisely what characterizes rationalism, as such, and Spinoza's use of it seems to mark him unmistakably as a traditional rationalist. To jump to this conclusion immediately, however, would be rash and we shall see presently that it would be at best a half-truth, for Spinoza's conception of deduction diverges significantly from the traditional Aristotelian conception, as it does also from that propounded by contemporary mathematical logicians.

The traditional notion of deductive reasoning required that it should begin from self-evident universal principles and proceed according to strict rules. Particular propositions could never serve as premises, because from them neither universal nor other particular propositions could validly be deduced. The modern view is that a deductive system is one which, from certain initial formulae of purely general significance (either symbolic, constructed from undefined elements, or axiomatic and taken as primitive), proceeds according to rules of transformation, which are arbitrarily laid down for the system.

Spinoza certainly believed that his first principle was indubitable, but it was not a universal statement of the traditional kind, nor would he have regarded it as at all similar to the postulates of a modern logical system. In contemporary logical systems definitions are stipulative and axioms arbitrary. For Spinoza this is never the case. His definitions are intended to state the essential nature of the thing defined; they are what are called "real definitions" and his axioms claim to be self-evident truths rooted in the nature of things. Universals, in the traditional logic, were abstract generalizations and these Spinoza held to be mere aids to the imagination or mental constructions (*entia rationis*) to which nothing real corresponds. Accordingly no reliable knowledge could, in his views, be deduced from them.

> It is never permissible for us, as long as we are concerned with inquiry into things, to conclude anything from abstractions, and we must take the greatest care not to confuse those things which are only in the understanding with those which are in reality (*in re*). But the best conclusions will be drawn from some particular affirmative essence, or from a true and legitimate definition. (*TdIE*, XIII, 93)

Nor did he believe that geometrical deduction of itself could guarantee true conclusions, for he declared explicitly, and enjoined the editor of his exposition of the Cartesian philosophy (Ludovicus Meyer) to state in the preface that he did not himself subscribe to all of Descartes' opinions, despite the fact that it was Spinoza himself (and not Descartes) who set them out as geometrical demonstrations.

To understand fully what Spinoza conceived as deductive reasoning we must take careful note of what he writes in the *Treatise on the Improvement of the Intellect*. There he faces the difficulty that the search for a method might involve an infinite regress, because, in order to search, a prior method would be needed, and then another prior to that, and so on *in infinitum*. But this, he points out is not the case, because the search for and study of the right method is a reflective study (*cognitio reflexiva*); it is the idea of an idea. As he explains, to have an idea is *ipso facto* to know that you have that idea—it is to have an idea of the idea. So knowledge of the method is knowing about true ideas. But this is possible only if we have at least one true idea to begin with. Put slightly differently, the knowledge of the right method is an idea (or knowledge) of an idea (other knowledge) and unless we have some idea to begin with the alleged regress can never get started. All that is necessary, therefore, is to have one true idea and to reflect upon that, and the more complete and perfect the idea the more fruitful will be the reflective study.

Spinoza calls the object of an idea its *ideatum* (that which is conceived, or "ideated" in it), and the idea itself, he says, is the "objective" or ideal essence of the object, or *ideatum*. What the object really is in itself he calls its "formal" essence, and he asserts that in a true idea the objective (ideal) essence and the formal (real) essence are identical. To know something, therefore, is to be aware of its formal essence as an objective essence in idea. So to possess the objective essence is itself to be certain of the truth, and we need no further criterion because the truth is the measure both of itself and of falsity, as light reveals both itself and darkness.

As the objective essence of a true idea is the same as its formal essence, the idea of a perfect being will itself be perfect and adequate and will be the ultimate criterion of all truth. As we proceed we shall discover that this idea is itself the whole truth; for Spinoza's doctrine, although he never states it in so many words, is in effect the same as Hegel's that "the truth is the whole." The right method, therefore, will be to relate every idea to this ultimate truth, the idea of a perfect being, and to do so in the right order.

The idea of a perfect being can never be a mere abstraction nor could it be an inadequate idea. This follows from what has just been said, for an inadequate or an abstract idea would be an objective essence itself inadequate and partial, and so could not be the objective essence of a perfect being. That must be a more real and concrete essence than any other: its objective essence must be as complete, concrete, and perfect as is its formal essence. This idea of a perfect being is the idea of God; it is the idea of God's eternal and infinite essence which, being all-inclusive (as Spinoza demonstrates elsewhere) is universal in its scope. It is, therefore, a concrete universal idea from which all other ideas must be derived according to the right method. In the *Ethics* and in the *Short Treatise on God, Man and Human Well-being* Spinoza maintains that the conception of God's essence is that of his infinite attributes, and to these he refers in the *Treatise on the Improvement of the Intellect* as certain "fixed and eternal things," and it is from ideas of these that all others are deducible in a necessary order, as these themselves follow necessarily from the idea of God. But these ideas are neither abstractions nor arbitrarily defined primitive concepts, they are concrete universals determined, as will later appear, by the necessity of their own nature.

The kind of deduction contemplated is indicated in two significant passages of the *Treatise* which are worth quoting in full:

> With respect to order, indeed, and so that our perceptions may be arranged and united, it is necessary that as soon as possible and as reason demands we inquire whether there is a certain being, and at the same time of what nature it is, which is the cause of all things, as its objective essence is also the cause of all our ideas; and then our minds, as we have said, should refer as much as possible to Nature: for it will [then] have the objective essence of Nature itself, and its order and connexion (*unionem*). Whence we can see that above all it is necessary for us always to deduce all our ideas from physical, or real, things, proceeding, as much as possible, according to the series of causes from one real being to another real being, and indeed so that we do not pass over to abstractions or generalities (*universalia*) either to conclude from these to anything real, or from anything real to these: for in either case, the true advance of the intellect is disrupted. But it must be noted that here I do not mean by the series of causes and of real entities, the succession of changeable singular things, but only the series of fixed and eternal things. (*TdIE*, XIV, 99–100)

From this passage it is apparent that the kind of "deduction" Spinoza contemplates is one which begins from actualities and proceeds to other actualities—a process considered impossible by contemporary logicians. It is apparent further that Spinoza thought it possible because he identified the causal series from one real entity to another with the logical transition from premises to conclusion, and he did so because he conceived the starting point of the "deduction" not as an abstraction or generalization, but as the idea of a concrete reality, or eternal entity, and so a concretely universal idea. The deductive procedure, therefore, is the unfolding of the implicated detail of the essence of the "eternal thing," as it unfolds itself in a necessary causal order in Nature. For,

> an idea has objectively the same character as its *ideatum* has in

reality. If, therefore, there were in Nature anything which had no interconnexions with other things, then, if its objective essence were also given, which ought to agree in every way with its formal essence, it too would have no connexions with other ideas; that is, we could deduce nothing from it. On the other hand, things which have interconnexion with others as do all things that exist in Nature, are intelligible, and their objective essences also have the same interconnexion, that is, other ideas are deduced from them, which again have interconnexion with others, and so instruments for proceeding further accumulate. (*TdIE*, VII, 41)

For Spinoza, therefore, deduction is not what it is for Descartes, "illation" by a chain of self-evident steps from one simple idea to another, nor is it, as in modern logic, the transformation of sentences according to stipulated rules. It is the tracing out of real connections between actualities in a concrete system, the differentiations within which are ordered according to the laws of its own nature—that is, the principles of organization and structure which constitute its essence, or its character as a whole.

Causal order, however, is of two kinds for Spinoza and here he says explicitly that he is not referring to the succession of efficient causes that occurs perpetually in what he later calls the common order of nature. He is speaking of the ontological series of "eternal things" (attributes of God and their infinite modes, which will be further explained at a later stage), which are necessarily connected in a precise logical order. This ontological hierarchy he also describes as a causal sequence, but it is rather a logical and ontological order of priority. Elsewhere he refers to it as the order of the intellect as opposed to the order of the imagination, or sensuous perception.

It is this order of connections that Spinoza believes himself to be following when he proceeds by the so-called geometrical method. It is not, however, the method that guarantees the truth of the conclusions. The truth of ideas depends on their internal coherence or "adequacy," which speaks for itself. The method is only the manner of exposition. There is no question of a comparison (such as John Locke demands) between ideas and some inaccessible reality in order to test their truth. Just as an architect examining the plan of a building can tell without actually building it whether it will stand up and function adequately, just as the mathematician without performing experiments can deduce the existence of physical particles (e.g., the positron, or the photon) which nobody has hitherto observed, so the philosopher can tell from the coherence, completeness, and comprehensiveness of an idea its adequacy or truth.

To do this, however, he must trace out the implications and connections involved in the objective essence, and Spinoza thought that the best
and most rigorous method of doing so was the "geometrical method,"
which is quite impersonal and dispassionate, justifying each step of the
argument by reference to what has already been proved or accepted on
adequate grounds. Its conclusions can then be contested legitimately only
by those who can produce counter-arguments similarly supported. As
Spinoza's aim was to demonstrate a truth valid for everybody as for
himself, he adopted this form of exposition as the most objective and
universal in its cogency that he could devise. It is not, however, a very
unusual form of philosophical exposition except in the way in which it is
set out. Other philosophers also try, so far as they can, to define their
terms unambiguously, to make explicit any assumptions or postulates
that are being used as premises, to state their theses clearly and to make
their arguments as cogent as possible. Spinoza does likewise, but he
borrows from the geometricians a form of exposition which is in many
ways inconvenient and which many contemporary readers will think
unfortunate.

3

The Idea of God and His Existence

THE BEST METHOD, we have been told, begins from a true idea, "and we have a true idea," Spinoza tells us. To have a true idea is to know that one has it and to know that it is true, for truth is its own criterion and requires no extrinsic mark. Descartes had maintained that the mark of a true idea was clearness and distinctness (a phrase which remains obscure to this day), and Spinoza, while he retains this description as characteristic of true ideas, adds to it "adequacy," which he defines as "having all the properties and intrinsic marks of a true idea"—intrinsic as opposed to extrinsic. Another feature of a true idea is its agreement with its *ideatum*, or object, but that, Spinoza says, is an extrinsic feature. The real intrinsic character of truth, then, can only be self-evidence, for if the idea is true it is *ipso facto* known to be true—that is, true on its own evidence. But strictly speaking, for Spinoza there can be only one such idea, namely, one the essence of which involves its being or real existence. This is the idea of Substance, or God, of that which is cause of itself (*causa sui*), dependent upon nothing else either for its existence or its conception, and therefore a being absolutely unlimited, or infinite, whether in space or in time, or in conceptual adequacy.

That we have an idea of God, Spinoza is convinced, just as Descartes had been; but many philosophers, before and since, have denied that they have, or could have, any such idea, and have doubted that those who profess to have one can rightly claim that their idea is clear or distinct, much less "adequate" in any understandable way. Before we can go further, therefore, all these terms need closer examination. "Clear and distinct," as has just been hinted, has given trouble to many a commentator.

19

Descartes seems, in the last resort, to have meant nothing more by the phrase than logically necessity—that the contradiction of which involves absurdity—for instance, it is clear that the statement, "I think, therefore I am," is true because the denial of it would be absurd. I can think if and only if I exist. Spinoza does not demur to any of this. To say, therefore, that I have a clear and distinct idea of God, is not to say that I have a detailed idea of everything that God comprises, but only that I have an idea which is self-consistent and the denial of which would be absurd— that I understand clearly what God is and what is involved in (or by) his essence; just as to have a clear idea of an infinite number is not to have an idea of all numbers up to infinity, but is simply to understand clearly what an infinite number means and what the conception implies mathematically. So to have a clear and distinct idea of God is to understand what is meant by an infinite and eternal being and what that conception implies. It is therefore, no objection to the claim that we can have a clear and distinct idea of an infinite being that we cannot comprehend the infinitely varied detail of its content, for a clear and distinct idea involves only an accurate grasp of the principle and the essential character of such a being.

Now, to be infinite means not to be limited by anything else, just as to be finite means to have limits or to be delimited by other beings; and what is not so delimited must, accordingly, be all-inclusive, for whatever it excluded would impose a limit upon it. What includes in itself everything that exists is thus absolutely self-complete, self-dependent (for there can be nothing outside of itself on which it could depend), and self-contained, both spatially, and temporally as well as in every other respect what-soever. This is what it is to be infinite, and to understand this is to have a clear and distinct idea of an infinite being. To have such an idea, therefore, is by no means impossible; in fact, Spinoza argues that unless we do have such an idea we can have no clear or distinct idea of anything at all, for it is, he maintains, the source and condition of all genuine knowledge.

It is now obvious in what sense a true (clear and distinct) idea is "adequate." The true idea *par excellence* is that of Substance, or God, an infinite and eternal being, and that is complete and all-inclusive. Its adequacy, therefore, is its completeness, its wholeness, what Spinoza identifies with its "reality" or "perfection." So to have an adequate idea of God is to have an idea of that which is self-complete and perfect—in short, simply to have a true idea of God. Or, putting it the other way round, really to have an idea of God is to have an adequate idea. To say, therefore, that a true idea is self-evident is the same as to say that, in order to be true, it must be adequate, coherent, and self-complete, for such an idea leaves nothing open to doubt and bears its truth upon its face.

We have clear, distinct, and adequate ideas of other things only so far as we can relate them in the proper order to the idea of God, or Substance, that is, to grasp how they fit into the all-inclusive being of God—or the system of the world (i.e., Nature). To this we must return later. Here our object is to understand what Spinoza meant by having a clear and distinct idea of God as an infinite being—an idea which is "perfect" or adequate.

Even if we can and do possess a clear and distinct idea of an infinite being does it follow that an infinite being exists? For Spinoza this is hardly even a sensible question, because he says (in the *Short Treatise on God, Man and Human Well-being*) whatever we clearly and distinctly understand to belong to anything we can truly assert of it; and we clearly and distinctly understand that existence belongs to God. This proof is one form of the famous Ontological Argument for the existence of God which has been enunciated many times in the history of philosophy, many times "refuted," and again reestablished. In brief it is the argument that God's essence—the idea of God—as an infinite and absolutely perfect being—necessarily involves existence, for if it did not it would not be the idea, or essence, of an absolutely perfect being and so would be self-contradictory. Spinoza restates the proof, not exactly in this form, yet in several different ways, of which the above is the first and probably the earliest of his formulations of the argument.

To the modern mind it is not a very appealing argument, but that is because too much is packed into it for it to be fully appreciated at first glance. Let us reconsider what has been said above.

An infinite being is necessarily all inclusive and so it must be self-complete. Whatever is must be contained in it, for nothing can exist outside (without) it. This is why Spinoza equates God, or Substance, with Nature—everything that exits. To say, therefore, that God does not exist is to say that nothing exists which does exist, and that is absurd. We can thus understand clearly and distinctly that existence belongs of necessity to God, or Nature. To deny it would be to deny all existence, including our own, which as we have seen is impossible.

Is Spinoza's assertion that God exists of necessity no more, then, than the tautology that everything that exists, exists of necessity? Indeed no, for first of all he would say that that is false. No finite entity exists of necessity, but only an infinite being. What Spinoza is contending is that nothing can exist except as a part of an absolute and infinite being, and that the Universe (or Nature) is such a being. It may well be the case that we cannot sensibly deny the existence of everything there is, any more than we can consistently deny our own existence. But does it follow from this that we and other existents are all parts of an absolutely infinite being such as Spinoza takes God to be? The universe indeed is everything that exists, but the objection may well be raised that the impossibility of denying its existence does not prove that what does exist constitutes a single, comprehensive, infinite, individual, and absolute whole. Might not the universe be just a vast collection of singular things with diverse relations between them, the existence of any (or all) of which is purely contingent?

The modern answer to this question would appeal to relativity physics and the contemporary conception of the physical universe as a "finite but unbounded" whole in which all physical entities and events are inseparably interconnected.* Fifty or sixty years ago, metaphysicians might have appealed to a theory of relations as inevitably internal to provide a reply. But Spinoza's response would have been to point out that a vast collection of singulars, however many, could never be more than finite, for each must in the nature of the case be limited by the others and all taken together as a collection are still a limited set. If we assume that their number is greater than any we can name, however great, we still have only an endless series of finites, or an aggregate which is endlessly finite. No one of its components is sufficient for itself and none can be conceived independently, without reference to some other (for that is the nature of the finite—that it be limited by another); consequently, each refers beyond itself for the explanation of its being and its nature; and that on which it depends is again dependent on something else and so *ad indefinitum*. Accordingly, no *adequate* idea could ever be framed of such an aggregate, and any idea of the sort we might entertain must be inadequate and confused—and so false. It is, says Spinoza, merely an idea of the imagination, and not a rational conception of infinity at all.

It is on the basis of this false idea of infinity (or, as Hegel calls it, of the false infinite) that many who oppose the Ontological Proof rest their argument. The false idea of infinity does not imply that it exist necessarily, for the essence of the finite does not involve existence and the false infinite is endlessly finite and no adequate account of anything can be

---

* Cf. Sir Arthur Eddington, *The Expanding Universe* (Cambridge: Cambridge University Press, 1933), and *The Philosophy of Physical Science* (Cambridge: Cambridge University Press, 1939); D. W. Sciama, *The Unity of the Universe* (New York: Doubleday, 1961); Fritjof Capra, *The Tao of Physics* (London: Fontana, 1975–76, 1983); David Bohm, *Wholeness and the Implicate Order* (London: Ark Paperbacks, 1980, 1983).

given in terms of it, for an endless collection of finites is strictly unintelligible both as a whole (for it is not a whole) and in detail, for each detail is explicable only in terms of its relations to the rest. To give a rational account of any one of the particular things in the world it must be related to a systematic context which, as systematic, must in principle be complete (for no system as such can be merely partial). Particular things can be explained only in terms of the organizing principle of some system to which they belong. To give an adequate account, therefore, of any or all of them we must invoke an ultimate absolute system, the whole of which in detail need not be (and is not) known to us, but which in principle we must presuppose as existing complete. What Spinoza calls Substance, God, or Nature is indeed the ultimate ground of all existence and all knowledge of particular things.

In effect, this argument is what in traditional metaphysics was called the Cosmological Proof of God's existence or the argument from the contingency of things to the ultimate necessity of an infinite being existing by the necessity of its own nature. Immanuel Kant showed, quite correctly, that this proof is really dependent upon the Ontological, because it must appeal in its last step to the existence of a being which is guaranteed by its essence (its nature) and nothing else. This can be true only of an absolute and infinite being but not of a finite and limited one. Those who, like Kant, seek to refute the Ontological Proof do so almost invariably by pointing to the impossibility, in the case of finite things, that essence should involve existence. They then extend the argument to include the infinite and all-inclusive. But that does not follow, for the reasons briefly set out above.

Once we grasp the principle of these two proofs there is no need to recount all the other proofs of God's existence that Spinoza sets out in his various works. There are no fewer than eleven, three in his exposition of Descartes' philosophy, three in the *Short Treatise*, and five in the *Ethics* (one informal and four formal). It is hardly right, therefore, to say, as some critics do, that by adopting the geometric method Spinoza was able to make presuppositions that he did not substantiate, for this "assumption" of God's existence is the foundation of his whole system and he spares no pains to show as explicitly as possible that it is no gratuitous assumption, but is a truth which cannot be denied without total absurdity. His eleven proofs are all different ways of demonstrating the implications of the idea of comprehensive and infinite being as self-existent, self-sustaining, and self-complete.

The existence of an absolute whole of being—God, Substance, or

Nature—is the foundation of Spinoza's entire philosophy. It is a being which exists and can be conceived through itself alone. It is the source of its own existence—caused by itself (*causa sui*), and through it alone can all finite entities either be or be conceived. As it is absolutely infinite and all-inclusive, and there can be nothing beyond or outside it, obviously there can be only one such being. If there were more than one, they would mutually limit one another and none could be infinite.

We must next explain how Spinoza expounds in detail the nature of God and the manner in which finite things depend upon God, but before we do so, let us digress somewhat to consider why, both in his own day and ever since, he has been accused of atheism.

It would seem perverse in the extreme to call a philosopher an atheist who spent so much space and ingenuity on proving the existence of God and elaborating his infinite and eternal nature, as does Spinoza. So much is his thought permeated by his conception of God that Novalis called him "God-intoxicated." Yet because he identified God with Nature, he seemed from the first, and to many he still does seem, to deny the existence of any God such as traditional religion recognizes. Tradition speaks of a God separate from the world, who by an act of free will created the world out of nothing, and rules over it as does a king his kingdom. For Spinoza the Universe is the totality of all that is, and he identifies it with God, which for the traditionalist, is tantamount to a denial of God's existence as a separate sovereign being. Moreover, Spinoza denies that God created the world out of nothing by an act of free will, for reasons which will presently appear. This denial seemed still more to confirm his atheism, of which his talk of God was taken as mere disguise. Further, the God he speaks of seems hardly to be a person. How could the universe as a whole be a personal King or Divine Father, as traditional Judaism and Christianity teach? Spinoza said, in reply to the question of whether God had personality, that he did not know, for he did not know what personality was, other than a word used by theologians who knew what they meant by it as little as he. Nevertheless, he maintained that self-consciousness, thought (for all thought is, in his view, self-conscious) is one of God's attributes, and he argued that human personality is perfected to the degree in which it can purify its intellect from error and confusion and achieve unity with the intellect of God.

Moreover, the traditionalist also wishes to maintain that God is infinite, that in him as well as from him all things have their being, and that he is the creative and sustaining cause of the world. To maintain at the same time that God is an infinite being and that he is separate from

the world is, Spinoza saw, an inconsistency, for if God is one entity and
the world another (or a collection of others) God must be limited by the
world which excludes him, and so must be finite. Similarly, if he created
the world he could not have been self-sufficient and complete but must
have lacked something, to fill which deficiency the world had to be
brought forth, albeit out of nothing. Such a doctrine, again, implies
finitude and imperfection in God. Likewise the analogy of a king ruling
over a kingdom likens God to a finite being whose power is not his own
strength but is derived from the society which he directs. This again
conflicts with the idea of an infinite and omnipotent being which traditional religion wishes to maintain. In the same way, it is inept in the
extreme to attribute to an infinite deity passions and desires, implying
wants, shortcomings, and subjection to external causation, like those to
which finite mortals are prone.

Spinoza, therefore, seeks to frame a conception of God which is
self-consistent and philosophically acceptable. He does not deny the
existence of the traditional deity, he tries only to free the common
notions from incoherencies. That there is an absolute and infinite being he
is firmly convinced by the reasons already outlined. What the true nature
of such a being must be he then seeks to discover by developing the
implications of the conception of absolute infinity. These, he finds, rule
out many of the characteristics traditionally attributed to God. He
asserts, therefore, that the traditional ideas are the fruit of imagination
only and not of reason. He does not condemn them on that account as
utterly worthless, but offers an interpretation of traditional beliefs and of
biblical teaching which explains both their value and their relation to
what he holds as true in the light of reason. We shall return later to this
account of religion, its character, the measure of its truth, and its significance for the life of the average person, as Spinoza devotes a separate
treatise to it. First we must understand the metaphysical position on
which it is based.

Another frequent assessment of Spinoza's position represents him as a
pantheist because of his identification of God with Nature. Pantheism is
the belief that everything in nature is holy, that every natural object is
divine and that deity resides in all things equally. There is much in
Spinoza's teaching to support a view of this kind, but so is there in the
teaching of Christianity. Saint Peter claims (in Acts 10:28) as a revelation
that "nothing is common or unclean," and St. Paul teaches that "in him
we live and move and have our being" (Acts 17:28), and the Psalm
declares that "the Lord . . . is holy in all his works" (145:17). To interpret

Spinoza's teaching as pantheism, is, notwithstanding, as much a mistake as to regard Christianity as pantheism, although Spinoza invites the error by his use of the word "nature." Nature as identified with God is, for Spinoza, the infinite whole, but he speaks also of "the common order of nature," which is a very different matter. The second use of the word refers to nature as it appears to us—to our finite senses and imagination—what one might call "phenomenal nature." This is what the pantheist calls divine; but Spinoza views it largely as illusion, or at best a partial appearance of the real. He is far from identifying nature in this sense with Substance or God. He would identify it at best with the succession of finite "modes" or affections of Substance as they appear to us in time. Nature in the first sense which is made synonymous with God transcends this "common order" and all human experience, as the infinite transcends the finite.

Moreover, as we shall find in due course, Spinoza did not believe that all things are equally divine (or "perfect"), but that the universe consists of infinite "modes" varying in their degrees of perfection—as he puts it himself: "To Him [God] material was not lacking for creating [every-thing] from the highest to the lowest grade of perfection." This is an aspect of Spinoza's thought which is commonly overlooked, but if it is acknowledged he cannot be regarded as a pantheist.

Thirdly, according to Spinoza, God has an infinity of attributes, but physical nature, which is the pantheists' god, is only one of these. Spinoza's God is therefore a transcendent deity, much more than and quite different from anything a genuine pantheist contemplates.

4

The Attributes of God

SPINOZA USES THE word "perfection" in its original meaning of "thoroughly made" or "complete." It is then legitimate for him to speak of degrees of perfection; and, as he uses "reality" in the same sense, he speaks, likewise, of degrees of reality. The more reality anything has, he maintains, the more attributes it possesses (and vice versa), but he uses the term "attribute" in a stricter and more specialized sense than is usual, not as synonymous with "property" or "quality," but as the way in which the essence (or nature) of the thing is conceived by the intellect. Again, when he speaks of "the intellect" he does not refer merely to human thought but to intellect or reason as such—strictly, as will presently become apparent, to God's intellect. An attribute, therefore, is the rational conception of the essential nature of that which has the attribute, and the more real the subject of attribution is the more attributes it will have. Accordingly, God, being absolutely infinite must possess infinite attributes, each of which is a way of conceiving his infinite essence. Each, is, therefore, infinite in its own kind, but as each is restricted to its own kind, it is not absolutely infinite. Thus the essence of God may be conceived as infinite extension, but extension is something other than thought and is therefore not absolutely infinite. Similarly, God may be conceived as infinite intellect, but thought is altogether different from extension and so is not absolutely infinite. Extension and thought are each conceivable through itself alone, though neither is self-sufficient, for neither can be conceived except as belonging to a substance, that is, each must be conceived as in something else. But Substance is absolutely infinite and there is and can only be one, thus both extension and thought are its attributes. Being absolutely infinite, however, Substance has an infinite number of attributes of which extension and thought are but two.

This in outline is how Spinoza sets out his theory, but this doctrine of the attributes is one of the most obscure in his metaphysics and leads to insuperable difficulties. These we shall discuss at a later stage; first we must consider in more detail Spinoza's account of the nature of God or Substance.

Spinoza defines "attribute" as what the intellect perceives of Substance as constituting its essence—but this does not mean that an attribute is a mere idea in our minds—or even in God's. God's essence is *what* he is; it is how he is to be conceived, true enough, but his essence is his reality, his power of existence (as Spinoza puts it). Spinoza demonstrates at length that all things flow from the necessity of God's nature, by which necessity also God is cause of himself. God's power of existence is thus equally his causal efficacy. God's power, or causality, therefore, follows necessarily from his nature or essence. Spinoza says they are the same thing; God's essence is his power or activity. His conception of God, therefore, is not one of a static, "block universe," but of a dynamic principle of action. The various ways in which the intellect conceives the essence of God are all forms of God's activity—his various powers. These are his attributes. Thus the attributes are not things but powers (or potencies) and the entities that they create are described as "modes" under their appropriate attribute. Thus thought is the power of producing "ideas," which are called modes under that attribute. Bodies are modes under the attribute of extension, which must not be envisaged as an unchanging expanse, or inert mass, but as a creative power. Nothing exists, Spinoza tells us, besides Substance and its modes; the attributes are various aspects of the essence, or the powers, of Substance, in which, or by which, these modes are produced. The power of God in act is what Spinoza calls *Natura Naturans*; the resulting array of modes he calls *Natura Naturata*.

The modes which follow directly from the eternal and infinite essence of God are themselves eternal and infinite. Although Spinoza tells us relatively little about these infinite modes, they are of the utmost importance for understanding his system and the way in which finite things are related to the infinite Substance. Under the attribute of thought the infinite modes are the infinite intellect and the infinite idea of God which it conceives. Under extension the first infinite mode is motion-and-rest (today we should probably call it energy) and the second is what Spinoza calls the "face" or appearance—or, one might say, configuration—of the entire universe (*facies totius universi*). As the attributes are powers so the infinite modes are activities. Although they are eternal, they do not exclude change, for their dynamism is a constant process of action. In the case of thought this should be clear, for the intellect is not a merely passive faculty but is thinking in act, and Spinoza is insistent that ideas are no mere pictures but are self-illuminating, self-conscious actions. Similarly, motion-and-rest is physical activity, and it is the variation of proportions of motion and rest in particular regions that constitutes bodies (just as the intellect frames ideas). But the activity is nevertheless eternal, for ideas are of the eternal essences of things, which are not subject to time and change; and the "face of the entire universe," though it involves, even necessitates, changes and movements among bodies, is an unchanging, eternal configuration, a sort of permanent steady state of motions in dynamic equilibrium.

Extension, therefore, no less than intellect or thought, is indivisibly one. Whole and parts, Spinoza declares, are notions inapplicable to attributes. It is only the imagination of finite minds that pictures space as an aggregate of separable parts. They are not separable (though they are mutually distinguishable) in reality, for extension is a single, indivisible manifold in which every region is essentially dependent upon every other both for what it is and for the events that occur in it, as those events do upon one another.

Spinoza's silence about the infinite modes of thought may be due to the fact that he spends so much space discussing the finite modes that he assumed it unnecessary to do more than mention the infinite intellect of God as their ultimate source. We can, however, construct for ourselves the relation between the finite and the infinite modes of thought by analogy from the brief but enlightening account that Spinoza gives of the corresponding modes of extension. This he does in two different places, one in Part II of the *Ethics* (following Prop. xiii) and one in the 32nd letter. Simple bodies, he says, are mutually distinguished solely by the proportion of motion to rest—or, if you prefer, the quantity of motion and rest—in a particular place. A number of such bodies, contiguous with one another, transmit motion and rest one to another. If in a group of contiguous simple bodies the proportions of motion and rest remain constant, it may be considered a single complex body, even though some parts may change or move relative to others. Combinations of complex bodies give rise in the same way to more complex bodies (like organisms), and if we continue in this way (as he says) to infinity, we may conceive the entire universe as a single physical whole in which the proportion of motion and rest remains always the same while finite bodies move about and change in infinite ways within it. It is this constant overall ratio of motion and rest which is the "face of the whole universe" and it determines the internal finite changes: "as the nature of the universe is not . . . limited, but is absolutely infinite, therefore its parts are modified in infinite ways (*modis*) by this nature of infinite power, and compelled to suffer infinite changes" (*Ep*, XXXII). Thus "from the necessity of the infinite divine nature infinite modes (that is all things which can fall under the infinite intellect) must follow" (*Ethics*, I, Prop. xvi).

Perhaps we can best explain Spinoza's doctrine by means of the contemporary relativistic theory in physics. Space-time is here considered as a single four-dimensional continuum in which varying curvatures correspond to different fields of force. Or in other words, energy pervades the whole of space-time, its various forms and concentrations producing various curvatures. Extremely sharp curvature represents matter, what Eddington calls (in different contexts) a "chimney," or a "fold," or a "pleat" in space-time; and the total distribution of matter and energy determines, and is determined by the pervasive shape or curvature of the universe as a whole, which is a three-dimensional hypersphere without bounds, but having a determinate four-dimensional volume.

The pervasive curvature—the form of the physical world—corresponds to Spinoza's *facies totius universi*, the local curvature corresponds to the proportion of motion and rest, and that again constitutes the distribution and density of matter. The whole determines the nature and behavior of the parts, and all the internal variations are mutually determining in a single interlaced and indivisible continuum.

As extension gives rise to the infinite modes, motion-and-rest, and the configuration of the universe as a whole, so in the attribute of thought we have the infinite intellect and the idea of God. The infinite intellect is God's intellect, it is his power of thought in action. The idea of God is his idea of himself, his knowledge of his own fully differentiated nature. Just as the generation of bodies and physical events are produced by motion-and-rest and are governed by the principles of order implicit in the configuration of the physical universe, similarly the succession of ideas is generated in logical sequence by the infinite intellect and is determined by the eternal laws of God's nature as they are conceived in his idea of himself—of the complete system of his modes. This is all that can consistently be meant by God's creation. Whatever God conceives or understands, Spinoza insists, he by the same act creates. His will and his intellect are identical, and his will (or power) is the same as his essence so that whatever he does is the necessary consequence of his nature. Thus he acts of necessity—by the same necessity that determines his thought, i.e., rational necessity. But as he is not determined by anything except himself, he is in no sense *compelled*, and his action, like his thought is self-caused (*causa sui*) and thus free.

"Freedom" of this kind, however, seems to be incompatible (at least at first sight) with change, or choice of alternatives. Spinoza certainly denies most strenuously that God exercises free choice. There is neither need nor possibility for him to choose, because his nature is absolutely perfect and alternatives to it do not exist, hence his acts follow from it of necessity. But we must not conclude from this that Spinoza's Substance is a fixed and frozen plenum without life or movement. God's attributes are his powers and must be thought of dynamically. Their infinite modes are activities, motion, and intellect. The processes of nature are the expression of God's causality and issue from the nature of the whole. Yet the whole as such cannot change. It is eternal, not in time, for it embraces all time and all possible alternatives, consequently time and change (however we find we must conceive them) are *within* the whole—otherwise it would be less than infinite. To the question of freedom we shall return when we consider human action, but we may mention now that determinist though he is, Spinoza strenuously denies that his theory subjects either man or God to fate. Determinism, moreover, is of different kinds and Spinoza's is not mechanical determinism. As we have seen there are different grades of reality or perfection among the modes of Substance. Mechanical determinism is typical of one grade but not of all. There is mathematical, causal, psychological, and rational determination, and it is the last which is typical (we shall find) of man at his best. And rational determination (so it turns out) constitutes free action.

From God's infinite and eternal essence, therefore, all things proceed in a necessary order, but in two distinct ways, which are nevertheless intimately interrelated. First the essences of all finite things follow necessarily from God's essence and exist eternally in God; the ideas of them are all implicit in God's intellect. This is because an infinite being, having infinite reality, must be infinitely diversified and, as Spinoza puts it, "does not lack material for the creation of all things from the highest to the lowest grade of perfection" (*Ethics*, I, App.). At the same time, through the infinite modes in the manner just explained, God's essence (or the principle of order involved in the absolute whole of the universe) expresses itself in an endless series of finite modes constantly coming to be and passing away in a ceaseless succession of changes, each caused by the one preceding, yet all governed by the *Gestalt* of the universe as a whole. Thus the chain of transient causes goes back to infinity but in all, and throughout its course, the immanent causality of God prevails.

As the active and creative source of all things, God is *Natura Naturans*, (creative Nature), as a system of effects, or created modes, he is *Natura Naturata* (created Nature). *Natura Naturans* is God's power in exercise; *Natura Naturata* is the structure of God's being as self-created, that infinite whole in which all things are and through which alone they can be conceived. Besides Substance and its modes, nothing else exists.

God, Substance, or Nature is one, single, unique, yet infinitely differentiated whole and, Spinoza maintains, its attributes are alternative ways of conceiving its essence or power. Thus the modes in each attribute are, one to one, identical with the modes in all the others. They are substantially the same thing. Thus an idea and its *ideatum* are identical in substance, though they differ in attribute, and the order and connection of ideas is, Spinoza asserts, the same as the order and connection of things. It is for this reason that "objective" essences (ideas) are identical with "formal" essences (actualities) and that to have a true idea all that is required is to grasp the objective essence of the thing.

This doctrine of the identity in substance of the modes in each attribute has far-reaching consequences in Spinoza's system, especially for his theory of knowledge. But it is also a source of several difficulties, some apparently insuperable and some merely apparent. I shall deal with the former at once.

Spinoza's Substance is to be conceived as an infinite process of differentiation of a primal principle of structure, each differentiation (or mode) expressed in an infinite diversity of ways, corresponding to the infinite attributes. The attributes can each be regarded in two ways, as a form or aspect of creative power, and as a world or system of modes appropriate to that form of creative power. The first corresponds to *Natura Naturans*, the second to *Natura Naturata*. The attributes are not divergent series of modes all emanating from God, there is only one such series, but it has infinitely many aspects or characters, one for each attribute, so that every mode is one thing, but is expressed differently in each attribute.

A serious difficulty, however, arises concerning the attribute of thought. There is an idea in God, Spinoza tells us, of everything that exists. That means that of every mode in every attribute there is an idea. The attribute of thought, therefore, should be more comprehensive than any of the others, for it must contain ideas of all modes in every other attribute. For each mode there should thus be an infinity of ideas. But if this were so the order and connection of ideas would not be the same as the order and connection of things. The series of modes in each of the other attributes mutually identical in substance, each to each, would constitute, as it were, a melodic order, while the order of ideas would be symphonic or harmonic in character. If one sought to avoid this difficulty by maintaining that only one idea, as the mode of thought, was necessary to express the corresponding mode in all other attributes, that idea in God's mind would have to be multiplex, as each mode is expressed in infinite attributes, and, again, thought would be more complex than other attributes—two-dimensional (so to speak), while each of the other attributes would be only one-dimensional (we do not, of course, refer here to spatial dimensions). Again, Spinoza asserts that the human mind is aware (as experience testifies) of only two attributes, extension and thought, because our bodies are modes of extension and our minds (as I shall shortly explain) are the ideas of our bodies. But if every idea was that of its corresponding mode in every attribute, we humans should nevertheless be aware of all the attributes, which is not the case.

When Spinoza's correspondent, von Tschirnhaus, raised this difficulty, the only reply he received was

> that although each thing is expressed in infinite modes in the infinite understanding of God, yet the infinite ideas by which it is expressed cannot constitute one and the same mind of an individual thing (*rei singularis*) but an infinity of minds: seeing that each of these infinite ideas has no connexion with the others. (*Ep*, LXVI)

We need to understand Spinoza's doctrine of the relation between mind and body (which we have shortly to consider) in order to grasp the meaning of this statement, each idea being considered "the mind" of its *ideatum*. As each attribute is conceivable only through itself, the ideas of the same thing in different attributes would thus be mutually incommunicable. Even so, the difficulty is not overcome, because all ideas belong to the attribute of thought, and in God they do all constitute one mind, even if not that of a singular thing. Consequently, the order and connection of ideas in God's understanding would not be the same as the order and connection of modes in any other attribute. One might still argue that it was the same as the order and connection of things in all other attributes taken together; but that would run counter to Spinoza's reason for asserting that ideas and their *ideata* are identical in substance, for the corresponding *ideata* in different attributes must be identical in substance in the same way. There would, in fact, have to be a separate attribute of thought for each of the other infinite attributes, so that thought as a whole would still be more complex than any other of God's powers.

In the terms Spinoza offers us this problem is insoluble, but its importance is secondary to the theories he offers of the world of our human experience: of the relation of the human mind to its body, of human knowledge and human welfare, and of our relation to one another and to God.

The other difficulty (which is not, however, insuperable) that attends Spinoza's contention that the order and connection of ideas is the same as that of things, arises with respect to his theory of knowledge. In explaining the different grades of knowing, he asserts that the order of ideas in the imagination differs from that followed by the intellect. The question immediately arises which of these is the same as the order and connection of things. It can hardly be both, yet if they differ, there must be divergence between some ideas and their *ideata*. This appears to involve an inconsistency in Spinoza's theory. In fact, it does not, but we must postpone our treatment of it until we have examined his theory of knowledge.

5

Body and Mind

As THERE IS only one substance and all the different attributes express its essence (what it really is), albeit each in a different way, each mode in any attribute is identical in substance with a corresponding mode in every other attribute, as we have said. This is why an idea and its object is one and the same thing. Now Spinoza teaches that the human mind is an idea, or finite mode of God's attribute of thought. It is, he says, a part of an infinite power of thinking, and the object of which it is the idea is the human body and nothing else.

At first sight this is surprising, for we commonly take our minds to have, or to form, innumerable ideas of innumerable objects, among which ideas of our own bodies will be included; but we do not think of each mind as one idea of only one object; still less do we take that object to be restricted to its own body. Nevertheless, what Spinoza is saying here is very profound. He does not regard the idea which is a human mind as simple. It is a highly complex idea, just as the human body is a highly complex body, and for this very reason, the human mind has exceptional capacities which we shall presently describe.

In the mind of God, we are told, there is an idea of every body, so that everything in its degree has a mind, but whereas some bodies are very simple, with minds, or ideas, equally very elementary, others are highly complex and are capable (in Spinoza's words) of doing and suffering many things at the same time. Such bodies have minds capable of perceiving many things at the same time. Moreover, some bodies are capable of acting from their own nature alone without the concurrence of outside bodies and their minds will be to that extent more capable of understanding clearly. This description fits very aptly the nature of living organisms. What is specifically characteristic of them is that they are self-maintaining in a wide variety of circumstances which would be destructive of less complex bodies, and when conditions change so as to become less favorable to their continued existence, they automatically alter their internal arrangements to compensate for the change. In short, they act from their own nature without the cooperation of other bodies. For instance, cold-blooded animals, like inorganic bodies, depend (at any rate to a great extent) upon the sun's warmth to keep them at the right temperature. Warm-blooded animals, on the other hand, have an internal mechanism for maintaining their temperature at constant level, such that, if the external temperature falls, it modifies the internal working of the organism (speeds up the action of the heart, produces changes in the skin and heat-generating movements such as shivering) so as to compensate for the change. Likewise, if the outside temperature rises, compensating changes (such as sweating) automatically take place in the organism to maintain its own internal level of heat. This is one of innumerable examples of the way in which an organism of some degree of complication can maintain its own system, despite external changes of conditions, by its own internal activity without dependence upon other things.

Such highly developed bodies are those which are sentient, and the more developed they are in this way the more clearly conscious are they of their environment. Thus, in Spinoza's terminology, the ideas (or minds) of such bodies are more capable of perceiving many things and even of understanding them clearly. We may readily agree that sensation is the way in which bodily changes are registered in consciousness and it is on the basis of sensation by its continuous articulation and organization that we become aware of distinct objects as external and arranged spatially and temporally in the environment we inhabit.

Our consciousness is thus primarily the awareness of our bodies in sensation. It is through this and only through this that we can become aware of the world around us. The universe being an indivisible whole, of which every part affects every other, it is registered as a whole through its effects upon the human body; and these are felt in varying degrees of obscurity and distinctness, subconsciously for the most part, and also consciously as moods and diverse feeling tone. All our consciousness is an elaboration of this primary feeling of the body and none is independent of it entirely, not even abstract thinking, which not only involves feelings of strain and effort but which is operative upon objects derivative from those of which we are conscious through bodily sensations. It is literally true, therefore, that the mind is the awareness (or, as Spinoza says, the "idea") of the body, and nothing else. But this idea, as experience grows, becomes elaborated into a world of objects in relation to one specially intimate and ever-present body, which we identify as our own. All, however, are discriminated within the manifold feeling which is originally the feeling, or sensation, or self-awareness, of the body.

In our common use of the word "idea," the ideas of external objects are elements within, or differentiations of, this general diffuse yet variegated manifold of awareness which is the felt or (as some modern philosophers call it) "lived" body.* But our developed awareness of an external body ignores—as it were, bypasses—the awareness of our own bodies through which it is mediated. I see before me the table and the paper on which I write and I seem to apprehend them directly, but actually my vision of them is a complex of sensations of my eye and its retina which my brain somehow elaborates as external objects. A simple experiment illustrates this. If one sits in a darkened room opposite a white screen, with the right eye covered, and if a small light, such as a flashlight, or a candle flame, is rotated beside the open left eye in a plane parallel to the line of sight, a pattern of veins will appear on the screen which are, in fact, the blood vessels of the retina of the eye. Likewise, if I close my eyes and feel my pen in my hand, it is as much my hand that I feel as the pen. The perception of the pen is an interpretation of the sensation in my palm and fingers. But ordinarily I suppress this consciousness of my own body and focus attention only on the elaboration of it that I call the awareness (or idea) of the external thing, just as I ignore the glass of the window-pane, or of my spectacles, when I look at some object through it. Only in special or exceptional circumstances, when, for example, the light is too bright, or the felt surface too hot or too sharp, is our attention brought back to our own bodies. Spinoza is therefore quite right to say that the human mind is the idea of the human body and nothing else, using the term "idea" to mean "mind" or "consciousness." But, of course, it is a highly complex idea, elaborated into the consciousness of a world.

This elaboration is simply the awareness of the effects in our own bodies produced by the influences upon it of external bodies, and as each body is, in various degrees, causally related to everything else in the physical world, the awareness of the whole world is contained implicitly (as it were, germinally) in the sensation of one's own body. The "idea" in my mind of an external body is strictly the idea of the effects of that body on my own. If it is a living body it will have an idea of itself, which will be

* The German word *erlebt* may be translated either "lived" or "experienced" equally correctly.

its own mind; or more correctly according to Spinoza this will be the case even if it is not a living body. But the idea (or "mind") of a nonliving body is, like the body itself, so rudimentary that it will be hardly, if at all, capable of perceiving other things. A living body, on the other hand, contains more reality—in just what sense, we can now understand more clearly. It registers effects from other bodies more variously, or, in Spinoza's words, it is capable of doing and suffering many things at the same time; and thus its mind or idea is more complicatedly differentiated and can perceive many things at the same time.

Meanwhile, we must not forget that an idea and its object are substantially one and the same thing. Body and mind, therefore, are one in substance. They are not two separate but associated entities. The mind is not a wraith or spirit separable from the body. Nor is there any causation between them, for each belongs to a different attribute. Events in the body do not cause events in the mind, nor do mental events cause physiological changes. Whatever happens in the body has bodily or physical causes and whatever happens in the mind has psychological causes. Nevertheless, the latter are the consciousness (the ideas) of the former because substantially they are the same. And because they are substantially identical we must not think of them as two parallel series of events in separate substances. They are just two different forms in which one entity exists (or expresses its nature). When the body is affected in certain ways the mind feels certain sensations because these are the physiological events as the mind is conscious of them. Again, if the mind forms an intention to act in a certain way the body moves appropriately because that movement is the physiological manifestation of the mind's action. Just how this comes about, according to Spinoza, we shall discuss below.

There is one mistake we must not, however, fall into, although Spinoza sometimes gives explanations and analogies to illustrate his theory which encourage this sort of error. The difference between the attributes (extension and thought, body and mind) is not just a difference between two ways of *describing* the same thing. If I say that I see a green patch and a physiologist tells me that at that moment a certain pattern of neural discharges occurs in my brain, the experience and the neural discharge are the same thing (though strictly this is incorrect because innumerable other physiological events contribute to my seeing the green patch and it might be better to say that my whole body as affected by the light is concomitant with the experience). My report is one description of it and the physiologist's is another. So much is true; but Spinoza would not

identify my idea of the green patch with my description of the experience
any more than he would identify the neural disturbance with the physiologist's description of it. Nor is either description applicable to the
other form of manifestation of substance. In saying that I see a green
patch I am not describing any physiological event at all, but only an
"idea." Likewise the physiologist is describing not ideas, but modes of
extension, motions. The idea and the motions are one and the same in
substance but not in attribute.

The best kind of analogy is the way in which modern quantum physics
describes elementary particles. Virtually a complete description can be
given of them as waves of some sort (standing waves, wave-packets, or
the like) and at the same time a similarly consistent account can be given
of them as particles. But the wave account is not appropriate to the
particle behavior nor the particle description to the wave behavior. Waves
are diffracted, particles collide and are deflected; waves spread, particles
follow trajectories. Nevertheless the physicists are describing the same
entities in each case which manifest themselves in two different and
incommensurable ways.*

This then is Spinoza's doctrine of the relation between the human mind
and its body. One is the idea of the other, and idea and *ideatum* are
substantially one and the same thing. They are the same mode of substance each under a different attribute. "From these [facts]," he writes,
"not only do we understand that the human mind is united to the body,
but also what should be understood by the union of mind and body"
(*Ethics* II, xiii, S).

An idea, however, is not "a dumb picture on a tablet," it is the consciousness of its *ideatum*, and consciousness is always at the same time
self-consciousness. Idea involves the idea of the idea. So, as the human mind
is the idea of the human body, there is also an idea of the human
mind which is the idea of the idea of the human body. Spinoza says that
the idea of the human mind is united with the human mind in the same
way as the human mind itself is united with the human body. That is to
say, they are all the same thing substantially. What this amounts to is that
the mind is at one and the same time the consciousness of its body and of
itself. We have already noted the importance of self-consciousness for the
discovery of the right method of improving the intelligence, and we are

---

* It is of some interest that Niels Bohr points to the relation between mind and body as a
case outside physics of the principle of complementarity which he enunciated as applying to
the wave-particle description in quantum physics.

about to discover (from Spinoza's account of knowledge in the *Ethics*, Part II) that self-consciousness, while always in some degree present, is not always present in the same degree, but varies in proportion to the grade of perfection or reality included in its object. The degree of self-consciousness which is present, however, is the means or "instrument" of increasing both the amount of reality included in the object and the adequacy of the idea.

It is to the mind, its limitations, and the ways in which they may be overcome, that Spinoza devotes his attention henceforth and our next task must be to explain his distinction between passion and action, which is the foundation of his epistemological and his psychological theory as well as of his ethics.

6

Knowledge

T HE IDEAS OF all bodies are in the intellect of God, as well as the ideas of those ideas, and God is their indwelling cause. But the existence of finite modes, whether bodies or ideas, does not follow directly, from God considered as an infinite being, but only from God as "affected by" (that is, as expressed in) another finite mode. A finite mode is caused by another finite mode, the existence of which is caused similarly, and so on *ad infinitum*. This double causality of God results in two levels (at least) of perfection in ideas, which are the basis of Spinoza's theory of knowledge. The idea of the human body as it is in the mind (or infinite idea) of God considered as an infinite being, is, at the very least, an idea of the body in the total system of its relations with other bodies. It is the idea of the body and the changes which go on within it as caused by and adjusted to all others and determined by the structure of the face of the whole universe. But the idea of the body as a finite mode, and of processes within it as finite modes of a finite mode, each caused by another finite mode, are ideas of a very different sort. For they are inevitably limited in scope, and however far we try to extend any one of them, we are ultimately defeated by the unending regress of finite causes.

As so limited, the idea of anything occurring in the body is simply the immediate awareness (or sensation) of an effect in the body of some external finite cause, in respect to which the body, and so likewise the mind, is relatively passive. I say "relatively" because the human body is a highly complex organism and is capable of adjusting itself to external circumstances and adapting to external conditions. There is therefore always some element of activity—or response—in the effects upon it of outside causes. Similarly ideas of such effects, though in some sense, because they are dependent on external causes, they are passive ideas,

41

yet they involve some element of activity, the nature of which will presently appear.

It may help to grasp this distinction if we quote in anticipation the definitions given by Spinoza in Part III of the *Ethics* of adequate and inadequate causes.

> I call that an adequate cause through which its effect can be clearly and distinctly perceived. But I call an inadequate or partial cause that through which alone its effect cannot be understood.
>
> I say, then, that we act when something in us or outside us is done, of which we are the adequate cause, that is, (by the preceding definition) when something in us or outside of us follows from our nature, which can be clearly and distinctly understood through that same nature alone. But on the other hand I say that we suffer when something happens in us, or follows from our nature, of which we are only a partial cause.

Accordingly, in all bodily response to external causes, and similarly in all ideas, there is an element which can be explained by the nature of the organism and its mind alone—an active element—as well as something which cannot but which requires an understanding at the same time of the external causes. It depends upon the extent to which either factor dominates whether what is done is an action or a passion and whether the idea of it is adequate or inadequate.

The mind as the awareness of the body is in the first instance sensory experience, the awareness or feeling of effects in the body of outside causes. It will thus consist of inadequate ideas. These are what Spinoza calls ideas of imagination, using that term to cover all experience which is primarily sensory in character and not only what *we* should call imaginary. The immediate awareness of an effect in the body of an outside cause presents in the mind an idea of the external body (or bodies) producing the effect as actually existing before us then and there. But the body is such that (containing plastic and fluid parts) an effect may produce a change in it which persists even after the cause has ceased to operate, so that I have the same idea of the external body although it is really only the idea of its persisting effect in my body. Thus at one time I may perceive as actually present the body actually causing the change in my body, and at another time, the change in my body caused in this way having persisted, I shall perceive, as if it were actually present, an idea of the external body which is not actually present and may even have ceased to exist. Spinoza says that we take the presented object to exist as actually present unless other ideas experienced at the same time preclude its existence. Thus even if the idea is only imaginary, if nothing experienced at the same time excludes the possibility of its present existence, I shall take it as real, as I do in dreams or when I am subject to other forms of hallucination. On the other hand if something causes me to imagine, let us say, some distant place where I have previously been, the present awareness of incompatible objects about me will exclude the present existence of the objects in that distant place. In short, sometimes I perceive things actually present; at others I believe things, which I only imagine to be actually present when they are not; and at yet other times I perceive present objects and at the same time imagine others. But as the ideas involved are all ideas of transitory effects upon the body from external causes, Spinoza classes them all together under the name *Imaginatio*, and it may be less confusing to use the Latin word as a technical term than its English translation, which has a more restricted use.

The nature of ideas of effects in the body of outside causes will be due in part to the nature of the body itself and in part to that of the outside causes. But the mind is apt to attribute the properties of the idea exclusively to the outside cause. As we have noticed we tend to overlook the body and, as it were, to perceive through it, just as we overlook a glass through which we see other objects. Thus as a man wearing tinted spectacles attributes the color of the spectacles to the objects seen through them, so we attribute to perceived objects qualities that really depend on our own bodies, as much as, if not more than, upon the external objects. All colors, sounds, scents, and tastes depend more on the nature of our sense organs than upon the external bodies to which we attribute the qualities; and when changes occur in the body which affect the sense organs, the qualities change; but we attribute the changed qualities to the external bodies and not to our own. For instance, a person with jaundice sees external objects as more yellow than usual because unusual secretions of yellow substance (bile) in his bloodstream affect his eyes. Or food which usually tastes sweet comes to taste bitter because dispepsia causes changes in the contents of the saliva. Likewise adventitious effects upon the ear will change or distort sounds despite the constancy of the external vibration. There are innumerable ways in which changes in the condition or position of the body will alter the appearance of external objects and it is only after a certain degree of sophistication that we learn to discount these effects.

Consequently, sensory experience is made up of what Spinoza calls confused ideas. They confuse the properties of the external causes with those of our own bodies and often in a very bewildering manner. For instance the moon appears to the unsophisticated as a quite small luminary a few hundred yards (or at most a mile or two) away. But this is because its surface subtends a rather small angle at the eye. Or again, a distant mountain looks like a flat vertical surface, but that is partly because the perceiving eyes are differently accommodated to it from the way they are to nearer objects. For reasons such as these other philosophers have called sensory qualities "secondary" and have maintained that they do not belong to the external objects at all, but are purely subjective to the perceiving mind. Spinoza, rather more soundly, maintains that they are confused ideas conflating effects due to different causes and attributing them to the wrong source.

As such ideas are not clearly and distinctly intelligible from the nature of the mind itself—for the causes of the bodily effects are only partly in the body—the ideas are inadequate. Consequently the knowledge we acquire through them, both of our own bodies and of external objects, is inadequate and confused and they are a fruitful source (Spinoza will say, the only source) of error. We may turn, next, therefore, to consider Spinoza's view of falsity as characteristic of *imaginatio*.

There are three grades of false idea not all equally erroneous. First there are fictions. These are ideas about possibilities that we entertain but do not positively assert. We cannot feign what we understand, what we see to be necessary (that is, what cannot be denied without contradiction) or impossible (that is, what contradicts itself). But we can feign, or suppose, possible existences. At least this is what Spinoza says in the unfinished *Treatise*. But in the *Ethics* he tells us that really nothing is contingent and that everything is necessary. When we think things are contingent it is because we do not know their causes. Now this is the case when we perceive or imagine an object sensuously, for we take the object to be present before us as it appears to us without understanding the causes of the appearance. Such objects, therefore, we can feign, or suppose, or imagine as we please. We can imagine flying horses, men turning into trees, gods into animals, and similar fantasies.

Such fictions are, as it were, floating images that the mind contemplates, but does not necessarily affirm. They are akin to dreams and reverie and in themselves, Spinoza tells us, they do not necessarily involve any error. The capacity to imagine things that do not exist, as long as we know that they do not exist, may be considered an accomplishment rather than a defect of mind, especially if it is the direct result of the mind's own nature, or (as Spinoza says) "free."

But such floating ideas are never merely passively contemplated. As has been said, no idea is ever purely passive, for all ideas are activities of the mind. The active element in fictitious ideas is affirmation, in spite of what was said above, for though no full assent is given to the ideas, we do affirm something in relation to them. For example, if I imagine a winged horse, I may not assert that any such thing actually exists, but in my feigning the object I am implicitly affirming that the horse has wings.

If, however, instead of simply entertaining ideas of this sort I assert their existence in reality I fall into error. But the error does not stem from the actual content of the idea nor strictly from the assertion; because the content is the effect of a real cause upon my body, either present or remote, and assertion is characteristic of all ideas. It is simply that I assert the content out of its proper context. I am aware of the idea and I affirm it only as it appears to me immediately—as it is caused by God, not considered as infinite, but only considered as producing effects in my mind through finite causes. The object of the idea is therefore taken in isolation, torn from the web of relations which really condition its nature and existence. It is not really the idea as it is in God (although, as it appears to me its actual content is *part* of what it is in God), because it is truncated and is only a fragment or a mutilated piece of the adequate idea. So it is confused and inadequate and that is why it is an error and is false. But its falsity consists not in what it contains but in what it leaves out. Falsity is nothing positive, Spinoza maintains, but only privation. Accordingly, while God is its cause, in the manner we have explained, and although the positive content is in God's mind, the falsity of the idea as it is in my imagination, being merely privation of relevant context and limitation of my viewpoint, is not in God. Being nothing positive he is not its cause. Properly speaking it is not *caused* at all but is simply a feature of the lack or low degree of perfection in my mind—its relative paucity in reality.

The third form of inadequate idea is doubt. But this is more a consequence of inadequacy than a form of it. Normally we accept and believe ideas as we perceive them so long as they are presented immediately and by themselves. If, however, other ideas in conflict with the former ones or incompatible with them are presented at the same time and if we do not understand their causes—either what has caused us to have them or what are the causes of the objects revealed—our minds vacillate and we do not know what to affirm. This state of vacillation and wavering of the mind is doubt.

For example, an uneducated farm laborer will believe that the sun is 200 yards away because that is how it appears to him. But, if somebody tells him that our senses sometimes deceive us and that the sun is really millions of miles away, presented with these two incompatible ideas, neither of which he understands, he will not know what to believe and his mind will vacillate in a state of suspension or doubt.

The greater part of human experience is confined to what Spinoza calls *imaginatio*. Our common unscientific beliefs about the things in the world around us as well as most of our religious beliefs are the products of *imaginatio*. Our emotions are for the most part reactions to imaginal ideas and our behavior is the expression of these emotions. To these common beliefs and the conduct based upon them we shall presently turn. They bulk large in the experience of mankind but they do not exhaust that experience, for not all human ideas are inadequate and there are available to us ways and means of attaining the truth. In fact, the truth is already implicit in our imaginal ideas because their positive content is in God, their causes are available to our ken, and their relations to other ideas are not altogether hidden but can be developed by thinking in the right order.

Let us first consider how we can progress from inadequate to adequate ideas and what, according to Spinoza, is the nature of the latter. Then we may give some description of common beliefs and the emotions and behavior they prompt, before turning to a discussion of man's true welfare and how he can attain to it.

In all ideas and objects, which, we must remember, are really the same things, there are certain common elements, common (Spinoza says) both to the whole and to the part. He is not referring to what some philosophers have called common properties, not those common characteristics with the help of which we form general concepts of things. They are, in short, not class concepts. This is an important point, and to prevent confusion let me dwell on it a little.

A class concept is usually conceived as a mark or property common to all the members of a group of things, which enables us to classify them as belonging to one kind and give them a common name. The class of things called mammals all suckle their young, the class of plants called dicotyledon are those the seeds of which have two primary leaves. Thus we form ideas in our minds of classes consisting of the common salient features of their members. Such ideas, in Spinoza's opinion, are confused conflations of images too numerous to be retained in detail, as the effects on the body from the objects concerned are superimposed and blurred. We perceive innumerable mammals, our memories cannot preserve all the manifold details of the nature of each individual but the images become, as it were, superimposed, like a composite photograph, and those characteristics which are most noticeable stand out and are remembered; then they are used as a distinguishing mark of the class—a kind of mnemonic. Hence we define mammals as animals that suckle their young. So with the rest of our general terms. We learn from them nothing significant about the essence, or true nature, of the things themselves. At best they are aids to the imagination and do not constitute genuine knowledge.

On the other hand, all things are modes of Substance under one or other attribute, and the characteristics of the attribute are all-pervasive within it. They pertain equally to the whole and to every part of any finite mode. Thus all bodies are extended as wholes and in every part and the characteristics of extension are universal to them. So likewise are all ideas subject to logical laws whatever their objects may be. Less obviously, but no less truly, all bodies, all physical events, as wholes and in all their parts must conform to the structural principles of the physical universe—*facies totius universi*. The attributes and their infinite modes are "the fixed and eternal things" of which Spinoza says in the *Tractatus* that "although they are individuals, on account of their presence everywhere, and their widespread power, serve for us as universals, or kinds of definitions of mutable singular things and the proximate causes of all things."

It is only by relating particular objects to these "fixed and eternal things," and by understanding mutable things according to the principles implicit in the eternal, which determine the true order of finite entities, that we can acquire adequate knowledge.

The "fixed and eternal things," however, the attributes and their infinite modes are ubiquitous; they characterize equally wholes and parts. The ideas we have of them, therefore, must be the same in our minds as they are in God's, and cannot fail to be adequate and true. Such ideas and their concatenation, according to the laws implicit in the eternal things—"as if inscribed in their true codes" (as Spinoza puts it)—constitute the second kind of knowledge, called *ratio* or reason. Here again we must use the Latin word as a technical term, because not only do we use "reason" in a looser and wider sense, but also Spinoza tends to use it sometimes to include also the third kind of knowledge, to which *ratio* naturally leads.

As *ratio* is concerned with what is common to all, what is in the whole equally with the part (as, according to *Lemma* II in *Ethics* II, all bodies agree in belonging to one and the same attribute), and as the universals with which we are here concerned are "fixed and eternal things," *ratio* regards things as necessary and not contingent, with the necessity of the eternal nature of God, from which the eternal things follow directly. It is therefore of the nature of reason, Spinoza maintains, to perceive things under a certain form of eternity (*sub specie aeternitatis*). It is only *imaginatio* that perceives them as contingent and under the form of time. But this view, if taken without qualification, gives rise to difficulties concerning the nature of time and its relation to eternity with which we shall have to wrestle in due course.

As already observed, the eternal things are at once individuals and universals. They are systematically structured wholes of which the finite modes are parts. This terminology, however, is only approximately right, for Spinoza, though he frequently uses it himself, warns us that whole and part is really a notion used only by the imagination. The eternal things are not divisible into parts. Their "parts," though distinguishable, are integral to the wholes as the wholes are determinant of the "parts." It would be more correct to call the parts "moments" within a complex unity.

Properly to understand any finite being, therefore, to comprehend it as it really is, we must see it in the light of and in its setting in the totality to which it is integral. The "whole" is logically (and in every way) prior to the "part." That is why Spinoza warns us against the uncritical use of these terms. Normally, we tend to think of wholes as made up out of their parts which we take as prior and more original. This is not true of Substance and its attributes, or of their infinite and finite modes.

The highest and best kind of knowledge, then, will be that which "proceeds from the adequate idea of the formal essence of a certain attribute of God to an adequate awareness of the essence of things." This kind of knowledge is called *scientia intuitiva* (intuitive science). It is "intuitive" because, once we have it, we grasp at once and as a whole the essence of things in their mutual dependence and their dependence upon God as their immanent cause. We comprehend them as expressions, or differentiations, of God's essence. It is *not* "intuitive" in the sense of being inexplicable, occult, or mystical; for it is the clearest, most distinctly discursive, articulated, and comprehensive knowledge possible. Intuition here is to be understood rather as insight than as intimation. By it we know clearly and distinctly, precisely and intelligently. *Scientia intuitiva* is not below or less than reason, but beyond it. It is reason raised to its highest power, the intellect functioning with consummate efficiency, the ultimate grasp of reality as it is in the intellect of God.

7

The Common Order of Nature

EVERYTHING IN REALITY happens according to the eternal laws of nature, everything is determined and nothing is really contingent. But the human body is only one finite mode of extension. It encounters innumerable other bodies which affect it in diverse ways. These encounters occur according to the laws of nature, but the ideas of them in the human mind are (in the first instance) only the ideas of the effects produced in the body. Their more remote causes and multifarious relations in the physical world for the most part escape the human consciousness, or are registered there only in dim and confused ways. The same is true even of the complex processes within the body themselves. They are all felt by the mind or color our consciousness in some, often very obscure, ways; but they are not revealed to us in their precise and detailed character, but only confusedly.

Accordingly, the occurrence of ideas in our minds appears to us fortuitous and haphazard. We link them together according to accidental connections. If two are similar we associate them so that the occurrence of one recalls the other, though they may have no other actual connection. Again, if one follows another closely, especially if this occurs frequently, although each may be the result of quite different and unconnected causes, we tend again to associate them and attribute the occurrence of one to the occurrence of the other. Again if we repeatedly experience certain events in conjunction and then on some occasion one of them fails to appear (for whatever reason), our expectations are disappointed and we alternate our beliefs about the causes of the aberrant event. For instance, if I see Peter every morning, Paul each noon and

James every evening, repeatedly for several days, I come to expect them in that order. But if on one day James appears in the morning, Peter at noon and Paul in the evening, I do not know whom to expect next. So I imagine such events to be contingent.

In consequence of all this the sequence of events as it occurs in *imaginatio* and as the imagination links them together in memory and anticipation, because imaginal ideas are fragmentary and isolated from their full context, is haphazard and relatively random. This is not because the ideas have no causes or are themselves fortuitous, but because their true connections do not appear to us.

So we build up in our minds a picture of the world in which we link together things and occurrences according to rough and ready rules suggested by common experience—what we call empirical rules. These serve us quite well for most practical purposes and the result is the commonsense conception of the world. It may be ordered even more regularly by inductive inference from frequent conjunctions of events, in the manner of natural history, and what we get is what Spinoza calls "the common order of nature." It is not the true order of nature—although, in one sense, it is part of it—not even within the limits of the physical world. Much less is it *Natura Naturata*, which is the whole panoply of modes in all the infinite attributes.

Viewing things in the common order by means of *imaginatio*, we see them as spread out in space and as successive in time, and we think (confusedly) of space and time as divisible into parts. We then compare these parts, invent measures of length and duration, and count things as separate units if they appear to us to be separated and disconnected. Further we group together things which are similar in more or less superficial ways, and form general ideas of them as classes; and we count the members of the classes. As a result we develop ideas of time, measure and number, which are, according to Spinoza, simply aids to the imagination. When we come to try to apply them to the infinite and eternal things we become involved in insoluble paradoxes. We ask if space goes on forever or has some ultimate limit. Then we see that if there were a limit to space we should have to postulate further space beyond the limit; and if we do that we can never conceive the world as a whole. But worse, space is continuous, so however small we make our divisions within it, there are other divisions between them. Space is infinitely divisible. Thus its ultimate parts must be infinitesimal, that is, without finite magnitude. But, if so, they cannot be aggregated to constitute any finite magnitude. For zeros do not add up to more than zero. Or, alternatively, if the ultimate parts of space have finite magnitude, and there are infinitely many in any finite length we wish to choose, every finite length will have to be infinite in magnitude. If then, in desperation, we say that space has no ultimate parts, we can no longer divide and measure it because we can find no stable unit. Similar conundrums can be generated with respect to time. But all this, Spinoza holds, is only because time, measure, and number are being used only as aids to the imagination, and the eternal essences of things, Substance and its infinite modes, are not understood by the intellect.

The puzzles arise, he says, first because we try to imagine infinity instead of understanding or conceiving it, and secondly because we fail to distinguish between what is infinite in its own nature and what is infinite only through its cause.* Substance is its own cause, its essence involves existence, it is whole and self-sufficient. But finite things are not and their essences do not involve existence. Each follows from a finite cause and that from another. The series of causes cannot be exhausted because it springs originally from the infinite essence of God (or Substance). The series is infinite only because of its cause, it is not infinite in itself. As we have seen, it is an endless series of finites.

It is to this endless series of finites that our finite existence belongs, and it is the way in which it appears to *imaginatio* that constitutes the common order of nature. But we can now see that although to *imaginatio* this order is largely appearance, there is a sense in which it is also real and follows from the nature of Substance. The endless succession of finite modes is the necessary differentiation of God's infinite and eternal essence under one or other of his infinite attributes, and it is within this succession that those events occur in the human body which are perceived (or sensed) in *imaginatio*, so presenting us with our garbled notions of the common order of nature. The intellectual grasp of the true nature of the succession of finite causes would, presumably, be on the level of *ratio*, which gives us the natural and mathematical sciences of extension, motion, and rest, and the laws of physical nature.

We can now see how to resolve the second difficulty we raised earlier about the order and connection of ideas. The order of the intellect is indeed the same as that of things. But the order and connection of ideas in the intellect is that of adequate ideas, which include in their positive content that of inadequate ideas. The concatenation of ideas in *imaginatio*, however, is the same as that of events in the human body and that is

_____
* Cf. *Ep*, XII.

part of the order of all physical events and is determined by definite causes according to the laws of nature. Only in our finite and inadequate thinking does this order seem fortuitous and contingent to us; but the reason for that seeming also becomes clear in the adequate ideas of the objects concerned. For then we can see how the order and concatenation of *imaginatio* is determined by that of causes and effects in our bodies. It is therefore true that the order and connection of all ideas, whether of *imaginatio* or of *ratio* is the same as the order and connection of things, and the succession of causes both in extension and in thought is the same.

8

Time and Eternity

THE RATIONAL CONCEPTION of nature will be concerned primarily with the existence of things as they are eternally in God, or as they follow necessarily from his eternal essence. The mathematical sciences of motion and rest deduce their propositions as eternal truths. The motion they envisage is ideal motion, not motion as we perceive it in *imaginatio*, as something enduring for a certain time. Time for these sciences again is ideal. It is not passage so much as an eternal dimension of events occurring in space-time, under the form of extension. They conceive it under a certain form of eternity.

How then are we to understand the nature of time, or duration, in Spinoza's system? For finite things do not exist by virtue of their own essence; to exist they require an external cause. We can conceive them as not existing, and their existence now does not entail that they should exist at any other time. What determines whether and when they exist are their finite causes; and as these are successive and are themselves dependent on other causes, each finite thing, besides its eternal being in the essence of God, endures for some finite time. Duration, Spinoza says, is a certain quantity of existence abstractly conceived, and it is the measure of this quantity that we call time, whereas eternity characterises "existence itself."* Here we have a problem of understanding the relation between, on the one hand, time and duration, "existence abstractly conceived," and eternity, on the other, "existence itself." This is one of the most difficult problems in Spinoza's philosophy.

The distinction between eternity and duration is a distinction between two senses of "existence." An infinite, self-caused being is self-existent

---

* Cf. *Ethics*, II, xlv, S.

and so eternal. There is not one time at which it exists and another time at which it does not; and while there is a sense in which it exists at all times, it is more accurate to say that, being independent of outside causes, it exists independently of time. Spinoza expresses this by saying that God has an infinite power of existing—an infinite power which is one aspect of his infinite perfection, or absolute completeness.

Finite things, on the other hand, have, in varying degrees, only a limited amount of perfection, and correspondingly limited power of existence. Not being self-existent they depend upon external causes to bring them into being and to maintain them in being. Similarly, as the result of external causes, they cease to exist. Their existences and the causes which produce and destroy them constitute a succession of changes, and the duration of each is a kind of quantity of existence. It is not identical with but has a relation to the degree of "reality" or perfection of the enduring thing, for the more perfection it has the greater will be its self-sufficiency, its power of existing independently of external causes.

The succession of finite causes goes on indefinitely. In terms of it we measure time and duration, the amount or quantity of a thing's existence, but we cannot add up all finite durations into one sum, because infinity is not an amount or a quantity which can be summed. Yet all finite existence is "in" the infinite and all-inclusive being of Substance, without which there could be no finite existence; and it is in God not only for a time but eternally, for existence in God is "existence itself." What we have to try to understand is this eternal existence in God of finite things and how it is related to their duration. Spinoza says that it is the essences of things which are eternally in God, but this cannot mean only that the ideas of all things are in God's mind, for their objective essences are the same, in substance, as their formal essences, so, at least in some sense, their existence must also be eternally in God. He is cause both of their essence and their existence.

As the properties of a triangle follow from its definition, so do infinite things follow from the infinite nature of God; and the properties of a triangle follow from the definition not only sometimes; not at one time more than another; strictly speaking, not even at all times, in the sense that we might say the Niagara Falls spill over their precipice at all times. The properties of the triangle are eternally implied by its definition.

In the same sense the infinite modes of God's attributes (like the attributes themselves) follow eternally from God's infinite nature. Now we have seen that these infinite modes are structural principles or what, in

Aristotelian language, we might call *"logoi"* (proportions, mathematical functions or formulae), in themselves eternal, yet determining the order of finite causes and the mutual relations of finite things, as does the "face of the whole universe" the physical things and events in the extended world. These changes, these successive causes, producing and abolishing finite things, are all eternally implicit in the infinite mode. They exist in it in principle, or in essence. And this is the way in which finite essences exist eternally in God.

Eternity then is not a very long duration nor even an indeterminable quantity of time. It is not in time at all. Time is in it, but not *contained* in it as matches are contained in a box or months in a year. Time is *in* eternity in the sense that eternity logically implies time, as the nature of God necessarily, because it is infinite and absolute, implies an inexhaustible diversity of self-differentiations—modes of self-expression or self-manifestation. The succession of finite modes is real. It is not just an appearance to our minds or a product of our imagination. How could it be, for our minds are finite modes belonging to the succession? Time and duration are therefore "real" and follow necessarily from God's nature, but they are the form of existence pertaining only to the finite, which does not exist solely by virtue of its essence—the form of existence of the *imperfectly* real. It should follow that the more perfect a thing is and the more reality inheres in it, the less its nature should be limited to time and the more nearly it should be eternal. This we shall find does turn out to be the case. But we must not conclude from this that such a thing will necessarily last longer in time, for the eternal is not in time. All it means is that such a thing enjoys a superior form or quality of being.

Eternity, then, both is and is not "the whole of duration." It is, in the sense that everything in time and its duration are implicit in the nature of the eternal. It is not, in the sense that eternity is not a vast lapse of time including all duration. Time is the perpetual and unceasing self-differentiation of the eternal. Plato called it the moving image of eternity. Perhaps it might be permissible to say that *our* notion of time is our finite perspective on this incessant self-differentiation of the eternal, and then eternity would be the determinant of all perspectives and the principle of their mutual interrelation. Or again, we might say that eternity is the source and wellspring of duration in time, its constant and invariant ground.

9

The Passions

Everything, so far as it is in itself," Spinoza writes, "strives to preserve itself in its own being" (*Ethics*, III, vi). Its striving is its *conatus*, and it strives, he says, "so far as it is in itself," for this striving, or endeavor, is its essence, as it were, asserting itself. Nevertheless,

> The Soul that rises with us, our life's Star,
>   Hath had elsewhere its setting,
> And cometh from afar.

The essences of finite things, as well as their existences, are posterior to the totality to which they belong. What a thing is in itself is a mode of Substance, an expression, manifestation, or differentiation of the essence of God. It exists by virtue of a cause which is integral to the configuration of the whole universe, which again follows directly from an attribute of God, and the attribute is God's power. Hence the *conatus* of each thing is the power of God working in and through it, but under the limitations involved in its (the mode's) finiteness. For God's essence expresses itself also in all other finite things and they are each and all adapted to one another so as to conform to the structure of the whole of Nature. So far as it is in itself, therefore, a finite thing endeavors to persevere in its own being; but so far as it comes into conflict with other finite things, its *conatus* is limited and may, if theirs is more powerful, be overcome.

If a finite thing does anything of which it is the adequate cause—that is, which can be understood from its own nature alone—it acts. If, on the other hand, what happens in or to it depends wholly or in part on external causes, it suffers—what happens in it is a passion. In the latter case, it is compelled to what it does, but in the former case, it acts freely. Free action, therefore, is not uncaused or undetermined action. It is self-determination.

In his account of the passions, Spinoza explicitly confines himself to the human mind. He is not concerned with things other than human, except so far as they affect human beings. He has established and therefore always presumes the identity in substance of the mind with the body, but he discusses the passions as "ideas" in the mind, without noting in every case the details of the bodily affections of which they are the conscious counterparts. It is the emotions as felt and experienced of which he writes, and the behavior in which they are expressed. Like everything else, they are part of nature and follow natural laws; for human nature, he says, is not, as so many believe, a law unto itself disrupting the order of nature. So many writers attribute human weakness to some obscure defect in human nature which they deplore and weep over, or ridicule and despise, whereas it is the product of natural causes and should be studied scientifically. A rational examination of the passions, Spinoza claims, will reveal their natural causes and will enable us to understand how they may be counteracted, so that the disadvantages of human weakness may be overcome.

At the outset we shall observe, as is clear from what has already been said, that the human mind acts only insofar as it has adequate ideas, and suffers only to the extent that its ideas are inadequate. Passions therefore are inadequate ideas and their concomitants. But not all emotions (or "affects," as Spinoza calls them) are passions, and we must not imagine that adequate ideas are devoid of emotional tone. They are, after all, actions and in them not only is the *conatus* operative, but since it is the endeavor to persist in one's own being, and as action is what is determined by one's own nature alone, adequate ideas and action are the very goal towards which the *conatus* strives.

Some have maintained that Spinoza means by the endeavor to preserve one's own being, the "instinct of self-preservation"; but that would at best be a minimal expression of the *conatus*. It is a striving to persist in one's own essence or nature, and essence, for Spinoza, is nothing merely static. It is the amount of reality or perfection that a thing contains and so is its power of existing. This is only another way of describing its urge or *nisus* to persevere in its own being. And as what is done from its own nature alone without the concurrence of other things is free action, to persist in its own being is essentially to act. The *conatus*, therefore, is as much an endeavor to increase one's power of action as to preserve one's finite essence. Rather, the effort to preserve oneself is at the same time an effort to augment oneself, to increase one's reality, or perfection, or power of existing and acting. To this fact we shall return because it has important bearing upon Spinoza's view of good and evil and of man's capacity for virtuous conduct.

The endeavor of the human mind to persist in its own being is the idea or awareness of the same endeavor of the human body and is the feeling of appetite or desire. Spinoza uses the Latin word *cupiditas* as the general term covering both, but he explains that appetite refers more specially to the body, indicating bodily urge, while desire refers more particularly to the mind. He says explicitly that appetite and desire are one and the same. But we must guard against misunderstanding. Appetite is the nisus of the body towards some condition of itself and this is felt in the mind as a drive or impulse. Idea, however, is an awareness not only of the body but also of itself, and being aware of itself the desire in the mind is also an idea of the object towards which the urge is felt. It may make a considerable difference to the nature of the affect, or emotion, what the object is and how adequately or inadequately it is conceived, even though that affect is still, in the mind, the idea (or awareness) of the body's *conatus*.

Desire, in fact, turns out to be the general form of all affects, but primarily it has two contrary (and sometimes complementary) varieties. Anything which happens to the body which reduces its power of action (i.e., which weakens its *conatus*) is felt as pain; and whatever increases that power is felt as pleasure. Pain, then, is the feeling of a process of diminution of the power of action, and pleasure is that of an increase in the capacity to persist in one's own true essence—to be one's true self. Spinoza says that the second is transition from less to greater perfection, and the first transition from greater to less. The matter is, however, complicated by the fact that our ideas of our own bodies and of other things are, more often than not, inadequate, and what we may imagine as increasing our power, or what does so only in part or in some restricted respect, may give us temporary and specious pleasure, although in conjunction with all its conditioning causes and their aftereffects it may reduce our capacity considerably and be the eventual source of pain. Inadequately perceived, then, we desire it, but adequately conceived we should desire to avoid it.

Pleasure and pleasant objects excite desire as attraction; pain and unpleasant objects excite desire as aversion. These are the three primary affects: desire, pleasure, and pain; and the last two are really only differentiations of the first: attraction and aversion. These, again, accompanied by the ideas of their objects are, respectively, love and hate. All the other affects are complications and combinations of these, depending upon the nature of their objects and the circumstances in which they occur.

Pleasure and pain affecting only part of the body Spinoza calls respectively "excitement" and "grief." If they affect the whole person he calls them "cheerfulness" and "depression" or "melancholy" (*melancholia*). Whereas love and hate are pleasure and pain accompanied by the idea of an external cause, he uses the terms "inclination" and "aversion" for pleasure and pain when they are accompanied by the idea of anything which is only their accidental cause. The difference seems to be one of stability or otherwise in the sentiment. I have inclination towards or aversion from a thing intermittently or changeably, but love, or hate, is a more stable and permanent feeling towards a specific object.

A more important point, which Spinoza makes both in the *Short Treatise on God, Man and Human Well-being* and in the *Ethics*, is that while all affects are ideas, the cognitive aspect is prior to the affective and conative aspects. For unless we have some idea of an object we can have no feeling towards anything. There are types of emotion that Spinoza recognizes in which we do not know what their causes are and cannot attribute them to any definite cause, but this is because their causes are, he says, accidental—because they have some accidental association with the true causes of the emotions. A sound or scent which may casually have been associated with something for which I felt fear, or love, or hate will, when I next experience it, arouse similar feeling. But I do not recognize the sound or the scent as the cause of the feeling, so I say that I fear, or love, or hate but I do not know why. In general, however, emotion implies the idea of some object towards which it is felt; so, for Spinoza, knowledge of the object is of primary importance in the determination of the nature and strength of the emotion.

It will be clear from our account of the body-mind relation and of *imaginatio* that all passive emotions will be accompanied by ideas of imagination or sense-perception. These are governed by laws of association and so likewise are the emotions with which they are associated. What accompanies an idea of an object of hate is hated; and so also with the other emotions. But love and hate are transferable in other ways as well. The former is the feeling of pleasure accompanied by the idea of its external cause and the latter is the feeling of pain similarly accompanied; and as the mind strives to persist in its own essence or power of action, and as pleasure is the feeling of increase in such power, or of transition to greater "perfection," whatever is imagined, or is conceived, as the cause of these changes will be loved or hated accordingly. And not only will things associated with the imagined cause be subject to the same emotion, but also what is similar to it.

Further we desire that what we love should be preserved and that what we hate should be destroyed; so we love whatever tends to preserve what we love and hate whatever tends to destroy or damage it. Conversely, we hate what increases the power of action of what we hate, and love what tends to destroy it. It follows that we shall love what the object of our love finds pleasant and hate what he or she finds disagreeable, and, conversely, we shall hate what those whom we hate love, and love what they dislike. Our feeling of pleasure and pain towards these objects will be appropriate in each case.

Further, we endeavor to bring about the preservation of objects of our love and to destroy those which we hate, and to affirm, or believe, or imagine whatever will affect the former with pleasure and the latter with pain, as well as to deny the contrary. In this way, we come to imagine ourselves and those we love to be better than we really are and to belittle those whom we hate; that is, we come to be affected with pride concerning our own imagined virtues and accomplishments, with partiality or overestimation for those we love, and disdain or contempt for those whom we dislike. Pride, Spinoza says, "is a kind of madness, because a man dreams with his eyes open that he can do all things that his imagination alone conjures up and which for that reason he regards as real, and he exults in them, as long as he is unable to imagine that which precludes their existence and limits his own ability" (*Ethics*, III, xxvi, S).

The association of ideas and feelings produces numerous complications in emotion. Because we tend to have similar feelings towards objects which are similar, there are occasions when an object which has excited our hatred is imagined (in Spinoza's wide sense) to have characteristics similar to another object which we love. We are then afflicted with contrary emotions towards the same object, and, as we cannot harbor both at once, our minds fluctuate from one to the other. Such conflict and vacillation also occurs when the body is affected in different parts of itself differently by the same thing, which then becomes the object of conflicting emotions.

If the object or occasion of our emotions is present the emotion tends to be stronger than when it is not. What is past and only remembered, or future and only anticipated, especially if long past or far in the future, affects us less than what is present or near. Thus of two things normally equally pleasant or painful, the one will affect us more strongly than the other if it is present and the other is in the past, or future. Thus what is less desirable but nearer at hand tends to oust what is more desirable but only expected to occur at a later date.

Emotions related to things past, which we remember, or future, which we anticipate, are hope and fear, confidence and despair, joy (pleasant surprise) and disappointment. Hope is inconstant pleasure about past or future matters about which we are in doubt. Fear is similar inconstant pain related to past or future objects about which we are uncertain. If the doubt is removed, hope becomes confidence and fear despair—unless, of course, the removal of the doubt confirms the opposite outcome from that feared or hoped for. In that case fear will be turned into joy and hope into disappointment. In every case the object mentioned by Spinoza is an image, for only *imaginatio* contemplates things as contingent or uncertain so that they would be appropriate objects of these emotions.

Things similar to ourselves (i.e., other people) tend to evoke in us emotions similar to those which they evince, because our body is affected by them in much the same way as their bodies are affected by the cause of their emotion. So we tend to feel sympathy with others and compassion. When this applies to desire and we tend to want what others want and pursue similar goals, the affect is called "emulation." So we come to pity others and strive to relieve them of what causes them pain, a propensity known as "benevolence."

For much the same reasons we try to do whatever we imagine will please others and to avoid what they dislike. When this occurs with respect to the multitude, it is called "ambition," but when it does not involve hurt to ourselves or others it is called "humanity." The pleasure or pain experienced in consequence of others' actions we express as praise and blame. Following from all this we have a tendency to feel pleasure in the contemplation of ourselves as pleasing others and pain when we fail to do so. This pleasure accompanied by the idea of ourselves as its cause is a species of love, and its contrary is a species of hatred; but as love and hatred refer to external causes, Spinoza gives other names to these self-regarding sentiments. Self-love he calls *gloria*, which may be translated "honor" or "self-satisfaction," and its opposite is "shame"; but this refers mainly to the feelings we have consequent upon praise or blame from others. When we assess ourselves in accordance with our own ideas of our conduct, we feel what Spinoza calls "self-complacency" (or perhaps better "self-respect") when we are pleased, and its opposite "repentance" when we are displeased with our ideas of ourselves.

When we imagine that others love, or hate, what we love and hate the emotions are strengthened; and vice versa, if we find that others love what we hate or hate what we love our feelings towards the loved or hated objects are weakened. Yet if others love something which we love, and if it is something that can be enjoyed only by one person, we do all we can to prevent others from possessing that thing. Thus the same human trait is the source both of pity for those who suffer misfortune and of envy of those who desire or possess what we ourselves love.

If we love somebody we strive to ensure that our love is returned, for we try to affect whom we love as much as we can with pleasure, so that they will associate us as the cause with that pleasure, and so love us. And if we succeed, and the more we succeed, the more self-satisfied and vainglorious we become.

On the other hand, if the person we love is imagined to love another, we hate and envy that other, the more so the stronger our love is and the greater our conviction that it is not requited. Jealousy, therefore, is vacillation of mind between love and hate, between pleasure and pain, accompanied by the idea of a rival who is envied. Such conflict may also arise in other ways and its effect is to intensify the emotions concerned. If we come to hate someone whom we formerly loved, our hatred is the greater because of our earlier love, and again if we are caused to love somebody whom we have earlier hated, our love is greater for that reason. At the same time hatred imagined to be unmerited excites hatred in return, because we naturally dislike the ill that the person who hates (or seems to hate) us tries to inflict on us and we associate him in idea with our displeasure as its cause. We then act towards him accordingly and anticipate his reciprocated hatred. Thus hatred breeds hatred and malevolence breeds vengeance. But in the same way love normally excites love and reciprocation confirms and intensifies affection. If, however, love is not returned, the lover suffers conflict because he has cause both to love and to hate the same person at the same time.

It can happen also that one may imagine a person whom one hates to love oneself nevertheless and the conflict which so arises may soften or even overcome the hatred, and if this occurs completely the dominant love, as we have seen, becomes all the more intense; and as love is pleasant and pleasure is the feeling of increased power of action, whereas pain is that of increased weakness and incapacity, there is a greater tendency for love to overcome hatred than vice versa. For the *conatus* is always in the direction of greater power of action, greater assertion of one's positive capacities.

Successful hatred, which inflicts pain on its object, or successful revenge is never wholly pleasant, for there is always some element of pain involved to the aggressor. For we cannot imagine something similar to ourselves being afflicted with pain without some degree of like feeling. Conflicts of this and other sorts are increased and perpetuated by the inconstancy of memory, which at times recalls one aspect of a situation and at other times another.

Further, our sentiments towards others are reduced in intensity if we believe that they are not, or are not fully, responsible for the acts which excite our feelings, but they are intensified if we believe them free and wholly responsible, for in the first case we do not think of them as the cause (or not wholly so) of our pleasure or pain, whereas in the second case we do.

Because people differ in bodily and mental constitution the same objects affect them differently—what one loves another hates, what one fears another despises. If another fears what I despise I call him cowardly or pusillanimous, but if I fear what he disregards I call him daring and brave. These differences in the way different people react to the same objects is a consequence of the differences between their essences. The *conatus*, we must remember, is the essence of the thing asserting itself, and as essences differ so will the way in which they feel and react to the effects on them of other things. Hence the emotions of animals, despite a superficial similarity of appearance or circumstance, are quite different from those of humans. What Spinoza probably has in mind here is that the feelings of animals are less self-conscious, more purely appetitive, whereas those of humans are desires with a consciousness (even if more or less confused) of their objects.

Just as the subjects differ who feel emotions so do the objects differ towards which they are felt, and there are as many varieties of a given type of feeling as there are of objects towards which it may be felt. So profligacy, drunkenness (*ebrietas*), lust, avarice, ambition are all varieties of love for different objects, and the names we give to their opposites, such as temperance, sobriety, chastity, and modesty are not so much names of passions, Spinoza tells us, as forms of action of "strength of mind," which moderates emotion and to which we may now turn.

The feeling of transition to greater perfection, or activity, is pleasure, and in conceiving adequate ideas, of which (we have seen) the intellect is capable, we act. Contemplating ourselves as active and as thinking adequately, we cannot but be pleased and rejoice, and all emotions associated with adequate ideas are pleasant. To such active emotions Spinoza refers under the general name of *fortitudo*, or strength of mind, of which he says there are two kinds: (i) *animositas*, or discretion, which is self-regarding and is the desire to preserve one's being solely by the direction of reason, and (ii) *generositas*, or magnanimity, which has reference to others and is the desire to help them and to unite with them in friendship.

These active emotions, however, are comparatively rare for reasons we are about to discover. For the most part men are the shuttlecocks of "diverse external influences and are driven hither and yon" by different and conflicting emotions, "like the waves of the sea agitated by contrary winds, ignorant of the outcome of their deeds and of their eventual fate" (*Ethics*, III, lix, S).

Of this passivity and comparative helplessness of man in the grip of external causes Spinoza speaks as human bondage. But prevalent though it is, it is not altogether inevitable. It can be counteracted and in large measure, if never absolutely, overcome. Man can free himself from this bondage and he does so insofar as he acts from his own nature alone. The manner of this liberation from the passions will be our final topic but it must follow upon some account of the consequences of human bondage and the measures which may be taken to mitigate its effects. This will involve a discussion of good and evil and a description of human virtue and vice.

10

Teleology and Freedom

BEFORE WE TURN to consider Spinoza's ethical theory, this may be a good stage at which to discuss his view of freedom—a matter to which he frequently reverts. It is a topic that has given, in the minds of commentators, a special character to Spinoza's philosophy, and yet his treatment of it has misled many (almost even himself) because he appears to make incompatible statements about it.

Freedom of will is commonly understood to mean our ability to do as we choose, despite external pressures and sometimes even in defiance of our own inclinations. So we believe we can freely choose the ends at which we aim as well as the means to attain them. Deliberate action is always purposive, for the sake of some end, and so has been called teleological (from the Greek word *telos*), and deliberate action by human beings is held to be free action. Freedom and purpose, therefore, and explanation in terms of the ends for which events and processes occur, teleological explanation, are all closely related.

Spinoza tirelessly declares that there is no such thing as free will, yet he speaks as often of free action and of free men. He inveighs against teleological explanation in all its current forms, yet he maintains repeatedly that nothing can be or be conceived except in and through God, or Substance. God-or-Substance is the whole of Nature, and its infinite modes determine the structure of the universe, explanation in terms of which (I shall presently argue) is the true and proper way to understand teleological thinking. Spinoza tells us that God does not act *sub specie boni* (in pursuit of some consequent good), for there is no end beyond God's being and action. Nevertheless, God is absolute perfection, and Spinoza also speaks of "the true good" for mankind. These are no mere inadvertent inconsistencies. Indeed, they are not inconsistencies at all.

Spinoza's fault is only that he never explicitly goes out of his way to demonstrate their mutual compatibility.

God is infinite and all-inclusive and his intellect comprehends everything conceivable; there can, therefore, be no end beyond himself for the sake of which he created the world. For him, understanding and creation are the one and the same; so it follows that everything conceivable exists of necessity: nothing is abstractly possible that is not actual. God, therefore, neither can nor need choose between "possible worlds" (as Leibniz later maintained), and there is no question of his having created the best of them; for all truly possible worlds are already comprehended in his infinite understanding and are *ipso facto* necessarily real. Consequently he did not create the world by an arbitrary act of free will and for the same reason there can be no human will which is free, in the sense of indeterminate.

On the other hand, God is *causa sui* (cause of himself). No outside cause exists which could either bring Substance into being or influence its activities. And to be self-caused or autonomous is to be a free cause. In this sense God is preeminently free, and God alone. Yet we shall find that there is a derivative sense in which human beings may also be free, with a freedom which is in the last resort the freedom and power of God. For freedom, as we have already said above, is self-determination.

But we must not proceed too fast. As nothing is contingent and God does not act *sub specie boni*, attempts to explain events in nature teleologically are futile and absurd—the result simply of confusion of thought (or rather of imagination). Man, says Spinoza, finds some things pleasant and others painful, and he seeks to possess the first and avoid the second. In the course of experience he finds some things aid his quest for the pleasant and his flight from the painful, while others impede his efforts. So he imagines that some things were created for his special benefit and others for the opposite purpose. Imagining God in his own image, man believes that God created the world and man for his own pleasure and provided man with the means of serving him, which, if man behaves well, will minister to his advantage and if he behaves badly will be used to punish him. Thus he attributes to God his own human passions and explains natural events in terms of his own likes and dislikes. So he maintains that Nature does nothing in vain, describing all things as if "both Gods and Nature were as insane as men." In Spinoza's view, such beliefs are nothing but a texture of superstition.

In much the same way, men imagine and speak of "an order of nature" because they find things easier to remember when arranged in certain sequences and not in others. So they say that God has set everything in order as if he had done everything for the convenience of the human imagination. Then they proceed to prove the existence of God from the order they think they find in Nature, which they see as evidence of a creator with an imagination like their own, overlooking the fact that there is also much in Nature which does not fit into their imaginary order, much of which they are ignorant, and much which they find inimical. But they explain the last to themselves as punishment for their sins.

When we do not understand the true causes of events and imagine them according to the association of our fortuitous ideas, we tend to explain them in terms of their known consequences instead of their unknown causes. So if a stone falls on a man's head and kills him we say that it did so in order to kill him. If someone objects that it did so because dislodged from a roof by a high wind, we ask "why then did the wind blow and dislodge it just at the moment when the man was passing by?" If another cause is offered for that, a similar question is put, until, says Spinoza, we are forced to explain the whole series by an appeal to the inscrutable will of God. This is merely explanation of the obscure by the more obscure, of the little-known by the unknown.

There can be no doubt or disagreement as to the unscientific and futile character of such bogus explanations, and Spinoza is right to castigate them. It does not, however, follow that explanation in terms of efficient causes is always possible or sufficient. As Spinoza himself affirms, we could never exhaust the series of efficient causes even if we could get to know them. No finite event is ever fully explained, therefore, in that way either; and we never could achieve an adequate understanding of things through their precedent causes alone. Spinoza believes, notwithstanding, that we can achieve an adequate understanding—at least within reasonable limits. But we can do so only by the third kind of knowledge, *scientia intuitiva*. This is when we proceed from an adequate idea of one of God's attributes to an adequate idea of the essence of things. In other words, it is when we explain the part (or finite mode) in terms of the whole, when we see the whole as prior to and so determinant of its constituents and not the other way round.

In the *Phaedo* of Plato there is a famous passage in which Socrates tells his friends that in his youth he studied the physical sciences in the attempt to understand things through their efficient causes, but he found this a hopeless task which shed little light on anything, for it seemed to him that the only proper way of explaining a thing was to show that it was what it was "because it was best for it to be so." This, on the face of it, is an advocacy of teleological explanation. But what Plato is trying to convey in the passage is that we could really understand things properly only if we could see them (as he says elsewhere) in relation to "all time and all existence"—that is, in the light of the whole. When people, as they often do, ask what is "the purpose of existence," they ask for a teleological explanation, but what they are really seeking is explanation in terms of the whole.

To explain an action or process in terms of a purpose is, moreover, always to seek to understand some whole or system to which it belongs or contributes. Our own purposes, after all, are not just the end-states of our actions. My purpose in writing these pages is not the last line or the last word I shall write, or my final gesture in throwing the manuscript into the wastebasket, or, if I refrain from that, my sending it to the publisher. It is the completion of a plan or design, the bringing of a pattern of action or expression to completion. Explanation of my behavior can be satisfactorily given only in terms of that design and that completion. This is true of all purposive action. It is purposive only because each and every detail of the process is directed or guided by the idea (whether clearly or only dimly perceived) of the whole design. Teleological explanation, therefore, in terms of purposes (whether God's, man's, or Nature's) are confused attempts at explanation of the part in terms of the whole. So what Spinoza rightly condemns is simply a muddled, mistaken, and misguided effort to do in the wrong way what he himself advocates and does in the right way—to conceive all things in God and explain them through God's essence.

This again is illustrated by his ridicule of the common ideas of an order of nature. He castigates them because they are confused and specious results of wishful thinking, ignoring or implausibly explaining away the plentiful evidence against themselves. But Spinoza himself speaks of an order of nature, and the whole account of his philosophy which has so far been given testifies to his conception of an order, rational and coherent, from beginning to end: Substance, from which infinite modes follow of necessity, modes which are ordering principles determining infinite series of finite modes. If belief in an order and explanation of its elements in terms of the ordering principle is teleological thinking, then Spinoza's own thought is teleological throughout.

But teleology of this sort does not exclude explanation in terms of efficient causation—quite the contrary. Efficient causation and teleological causation are complementary views of the same process, as Spinoza's account of the face of the whole universe beautifully illustrates. It is like the way in which embryologists explain the development of the germ cell, in terms of the specific character of the adult form which is being generated; but that by no means prevents them from seeing each successive phase as a consequence of the prior phase, its efficient cause. Consequently, mechanism is not incompatible with teleology, for mechanisms, as our own artifacts bear witness, serve purposes. They are all structured systems of parts that can be understood fully only if both the efficient causation of their working and the total plan of their construction, as well as their function, are clearly grasped. Machines made by man are teleological devices and mechanisms which abound in living organisms serve the purpose and function of maintaining the complex system or organic metabolism and bodily structure intact.

Mechanistic explanation does not, therefore, rule out teleological explanation; each supplements the other, and perhaps in all cases other than those involving only abstracted features of the motion of simple physical bodies, both are required. Consequently, it is quite wrong to interpret Spinoza as advocating a so-called mechanistic universe. He does maintain that everything in it is necessarily determined and that all finite events have efficient causes, but he also insists that they can be adequately comprehended only if seen in their place in the total system, through "an adequate idea of one of the attributes of Substance." Nor does his universe exclude purposive activity, for this is involved in the exercise of the *conatus* of all finite things. God, of course, can have no ulterior purpose for his activity because God is infinite, but his essence is, intrinsically and in every aspect and attribute, activity. His essence is his infinite power; and the *conatus* of his finite modes is its expression.

How does all this affect the conception of the human will and Spinoza's view of human responsibility and freedom?

Free will as arbitrary choice undetermined by any cause or directing principle, he rejects unreservedly. We believe that our actions are free, he says, because we are ignorant of their causes, just as a falling stone might imagine that it acted of its own free will if it could be conscious of its movement. Also, we attribute free will to ourselves and to other persons in our endeavor to think of ourselves as responsible for our behavior and to hold others responsible for theirs. But if we acted from a will that was wholly indeterminate our actions would be wholly unaccountable, altogether unpredictable and unreliable. We should then be totally irresponsible and could never rightly answer for any of our deeds. Our freedom could be used as an excuse for everything we did, and today some seem to think that they can claim it as a right which will justify whatever course they choose, however wayward.

Spinoza was well aware that the claim to free will was ultimately self-defeating, and he argued at length and with much emphasis that determination of action does not preclude responsibility—although compulsion does. Compulsion is determination by outside causes beyond our control, but not all determination is compulsion, for some action (action properly so-called) is determined by the nature of the agent alone: it is self-determined. The antithesis, he says, is not between determination and freedom, but between determination and chance on the one hand, and between freedom and compulsion on the other. Behavior which is compelled in the sense that it is determined by outside causes is neither free nor responsible. But action determined solely by the nature (or essence) of the agent is both free and responsible. Spinoza does deny the existence of a will which is free in the sense of undetermined or uncaused, but he does not deny the possibility of human action which is free in the sense of autonomous.

Such action is the expression of adequate ideas, ideas formed by the intellect unadulterated by *imaginatio*. And the intellect, whether of God or of man, Spinoza identifies with will. Free will, therefore, in the only acceptable sense of the phrase, is reason. So far from denying the reality of human freedom, Spinoza denies only what is an indefensible theory of the will.

This doctrine has interesting consequences for ethics. The sort of conduct which we usually call vicious, and which Spinoza (as we shall shortly see) also regards as evil, in senses to be explained, is conduct giving expression to passion; and passion is the feeling or awareness of effects in the body of outside causes. Such conduct, therefore, is neither free nor responsible, and to blame anybody for it is futile. "A horse is excusable," writes Spinoza in one of his letters, "that it is a horse and not a man." So the criminal is "excusable" for being a plaything of his passions. Blame and praise are themselves only the expression of passions, hence to say that a person's conduct is blameworthy is only to say that others disapprove of it, not that it is free. Nevertheless, it does not follow that the criminal's behavior is desirable, socially or personally, nor that it is to his or anybody else's advantage—quite the reverse—nor that it is to be condoned, for some form of punishment may be the right way to counteract it and to protect others from its harmful effects. If a dog goes mad, Spinoza writes in the same letter, or a man is infected by its bite, neither of them is to be blamed, but drastic remedies are nevertheless called for.

On the other hand, free action, which we shall find is action in accordance with reason, is both virtuous and responsible. It needs neither praise nor reward, however, for it is its own reward and being independent of passion, praise will affect it in no way. It is independent of passion, but not of emotion, for true action, we have been told, is always pleasant.

Spinoza's determinism, we may note in conclusion, is not mechanistic determinism, for he envisages determination of more than one kind. It may be mechanistic in the case of simple bodies, and mechanism may also be involved in more complex bodies, but in their case other principles may also be involved, so that human behavior determined by passion is on a different, and (presumably) higher level. Finally, autonomous action is rationally determined. It is free, and is on a higher level still. The determination of God's action, which is free in the fullest sense, is the highest form of all and is the source and foundation of all the other grades of determinism.

Now a series of this kind, of grades of increasing perfection (for, let there be no mistake, these types of determinism are correlative with grades of perfection which have already been noted)—such a series, in which the last phase is implicit from the beginning, immanent throughout, and sums up and sublimates all the rest, is what is called a dialectical series. It is the archetype of every sort of development process and is essentially teleological.

One must not be misled into thinking that Spinoza's philosophy is not itself dialectical in spirit by his polemics against teleology. The polemics are against muddled and low-grade thinking, and are well merited. There is a far sounder and much more defensible sense of teleology, for which some modern biological theories now substitute the term "teleonomy"; and in this sense Spinoza's system is essentially teleonomic.

11

Good and Evil

THE VARIOUS STATEMENTS about good and evil scattered about Spinoza's writings give the impression that he meant to deny the existence of values in reality and the legitimate use of value terms in philosophy. Such a denial, moreover, would seem to be entirely consonant with his general metaphysical position, with the rejection of teleology and the assertion that all things are necessarily what they are and could not be otherwise. Once again, this impression is due to misunderstanding, frequent though it is among the interpretations of Spinoza's philosophy in the literature upon the subject. The foregoing discussion, however, will already have put the reader on his guard against such misinterpretation.

Although Spinoza says different things in different contexts about good and evil and his statements appear at first sight even to be mutually inconsistent, careful examination will show that every apparently divergent statement has a place and fits harmoniously in a single coherent theory. The key to the understanding of the position consistently maintained is Spinoza's use of the word "perfection" as synonymous with "reality" and "completeness," although even that is somewhat obscured by what he writes in the preface to Part IV of the *Ethics*, where he explains that in common usage the meaning of that term also has relation to our imaginal ideas. When we think of artifacts, he reminds us, we form a notion of what the artificer intends, or intended, to make and we compare the finished product with that. If it conforms to the idea we describe it as perfect, but if not as imperfect. Then in the case of natural entities we construct (as has been explained) abstract or general ideas which we identify as their "natures," and when we find any which fail to correspond with our general idea of the type, we say it is imperfect; when the presented example does correspond with our idea we say it is perfect.

But this is only common usage founded upon *imaginatio*. It is not precise, scientific, usage of the word "perfection." The difference between *imaginatio* as contrasted with *ratio* and *scientia intuitiva* must constantly be kept in mind, for what are commonly thought and spoken of as good and evil, perfect and imperfect, are not by any means always so, even when judged by common standards. Inadequate ideas of goodness and badness are very different from adequate conceptions, all of which have to be sorted out and assigned their proper place in a consistent view.

Perhaps the best procedure would be to begin by stating Spinoza's main position as it should be understood. We shall then be able to see how Spinoza's various remarks about good and evil in different places belong to it, and how they apply without conflict to various aspects and levels of human belief and practice.

Nature, taken as an infinite whole, Substance, or God, is absolutely self-contained and self-complete. It is, in the full and legitimate sense of the word, perfect, as a whole and as expressed in infinite modes of self-manifestation. It is what it must be and could not be otherwise; and because it is absolutely whole and all-embracing, it is not, and could not possibly be, a merely blank unity without internal self-differentiation. In fact, its differentiation is and must be infinitely various. God, says Spinoza, does not lack material for the creation of all things from the highest to the lowest degree of perfection. The last word of this sentence must be understood in the sense explained. The degrees of perfection intended are degrees of completeness, wholeness, or inclusiveness of reality, examples of which we have already discussed. The infinite series of modes which proceed necessarily from the nature of God or Substance are ranged in a scale of progressively increasing grades of perfection from the lowest to the highest—that is, right up to the infinite perfection of Substance itself.

Simple bodies include a very small amount of reality in themselves and their ideas are correspondingly simple. But bodies range from such simple atoms through every degree of complexity, progressively increasing in inclusiveness, in their independent capacity for doing and suffering, up to the entire physical world regarded as a single organic individual. Their ideas or minds constitute a similar scale of increasing capacity to perceive and to understand. So we reach the level of the *facies totius universi* and the infinite modes of Substance which directly express the specific nature of each of its infinite attributes. We must bear in mind also that the attributes are expressive of essence and that essence is the dynamic power of existence.

This power, as operative in each finite mode is its *conatus* to persevere in its own being. We may legitimately presume that in simple bodies this *conatus* is a tendency not only or always to repel others, but, more appropriately, to combine with others and so (as we have seen) to increase the power of action of the more complex structure. Action being what is determined solely through the nature of the agent, the *conatus* to persist in its own essence is a *conatus* to increase its active capacity. This is the same thing as increasing its degree of reality or perfection. Whatever conduces to such increase in the power of action is good for the agent and whatever impedes it is evil.

In the case of mankind, power of action is proportionate to understanding, or ability to frame adequate ideas. Accordingly, whatever is instrumental to the improvement or perfection of the intellect is good for mankind, and whatever obstructs or reduces intellectual capacity is evil. The former, being of necessity a transition from less to greater perfection and being at the same time a similar increase in the power of action of the body, is felt as pleasure; while the latter, being transition in the opposite sense, is felt as pain. This is not a purely intellectualist doctrine, because body and mind are one thing, the felt transition is as much physical as mental, and all ideas are at once both cognitive and affective.

Whatever aids and brings to fruition the perfection of his mind is thus the true good for man, and what does so is pleasant. But it is not the case that whatever is pleasant does so. The body may be affected in part of itself in such a way that the mind experiences pleasure, while it is affected in other parts quite differently. Moreover, some such effects are not dependent solely on its own nature but are at least partially (and to varying extents) caused by other bodies, whose natures contribute as much, or maybe more, to the final effect. The increase in the power of action may in consequence be spurious, or at best temporary. We may thus, and often do, imagine things to be good, because we find them pleasant for the moment, which are not really to our true advantage (taken as the real increase in our power of action). We therefore come to apply the words "good" and "evil" in all kinds of inappropriate ways, dictated by our imagination and not by our intelligence. These uses of the words have very different values and significances from their legitimate use, as above explained; and Spinoza's criticism of them accounts for the diversity and apparent inconsistency of his various statements. We may now turn to these statements and see why they are divergent and yet not incompatible with the doctrine as set out above.

First, as they are applied to man, whether in the legitimate sense or in many spurious senses, the terms "good" and "evil" do not apply and cannot be applied to God. God is perfect only in the sense that he is absolutely real and self-complete. It makes no real sense to think of him as perfectly benevolent, for benevolence is merely a human affection which God, who is pure activity, could not feel. The "goodness" of God, if it is to have any conceivable meaning at all, must be understood quite differently, in a way which becomes apparent only in the conclusion of the *Ethics*. Men commonly try to imagine God as having human characteristics and propensities and so fall into the wildest and most ludicrous errors. In this fashion they come to believe that God acts for special purposes and directs all things for their own special benefit so that men may be beholden to him and do him the highest honor. So they devise numerous fantastic ways of worshipping, each according to his own fancy, designed to make God love him above all others and dispose the whole of nature for the gratification of his desires and insatiable greed—as if God were as imbecile as man. As applied to God, then, the terms "good" and "evil" lead to absurdity, but even as commonly applied to human affairs they frequently indicate nothing real.

In the main, men call good whatever pleases them and bad whatever does not. But different things please different people, and vary even for the same person at different times. Good and evil thus become purely relative terms, relative both to the person and to the circumstances. "For example," writes Spinoza, "music is good to the melancholy, bad to those who mourn, and neither good nor bad to the deaf." *As so used* the words refer to nothing real or stable and when made into substantives, when men speak of "good" and "evil" as entities, the terms have no intelligible referent. Good and evil in this usage are simply ways of imagining. They refer to nothing in nature.

Again, in common use, the word "perfection" means fully fashioned. A craftsman or artist making some object or utensil has an idea in his mind of what the artifact will be when finished. What conforms to this idea he calls perfect, and others use the word likewise to indicate that the object fulfils the maker's intention. It is "imperfect" so far as it falls short of that goal. Similarly, we form general ideas of natural entities, as has already been explained, by combining images and abstracting common characteristics. So we put together an idea as a sort of standard to which we expect the thing to conform, having all the salient features of our generalized image. When it fails to conform we say that it is imperfect, and when it does conform we say it is perfect. But abstract ideas correspond to nothing real.

On the other hand, men and women think things good according as they are pleased by them; and as things help them to acquire what is pleasant so they deem them advantageous. Such things they desire and whatever they desire they call profitable, and what they deem profitable they call good. What they find in this sense disadvantageous and undesirable they call evil.

This propensity in mankind to seek their own profit and advantage is, however, an expression of their *conatus*. For that reason it is not wholly divorced from what really is to their advantage. Though they may, under the influence of imagination and passion, pursue objects the attainment of which will not actually increase their power of action and will result finally only in disappointment, disillusion, and misery, nevertheless, in its essential nature, their desire is for what will increase the power of action—what will confirm each in his or her own essence—and whatever really does that is the *true* good. What this is one can only know with any sort of reliability so far as one thinks adequately. For what we imagine to be for our benefit is usually far wide of the mark. Accordingly, Spinoza defines "good" and "evil" in Part IV of the *Ethics* as follows:

> By good I understand that which we know for certain to be useful to us.
> By evil, however, that which we know for certain hinders us from the possession of good.

We know for certain only when we think adequately, only when our knowledge is rational and of the second and third kinds. What we imagine to be useful to us, though we call it good, is not necessarily if ever really good, as Spinoza here defines the term.

Man under the influence of the passions is a prey to conflicts of emotion, vacillation of mind, envy, hatred, betrayal, disappointment, and every sort of injury and misfortune. He is swept this way and that "like the waves of the sea agitated by contrary winds." But he is capable, in ways we are yet to discover, of overcoming the passions and rising above the vicissitudes of fortune. At all events we can without difficulty conceive a condition of man much superior to his common lot, and a character which would be far stabler and more strong-minded than we averagely experience. Taking such a character as a standard or ideal, we can say that whatever is done and whatever serves to help people to attain it is good and whatever obstructs their effort to do so is not.

This ideal of human character would, moreover, be one in which the power of action is maximized. The use of the terms good and evil with reference to this ideal or standard is therefore sound and legitimate. Such an ideal Spinoza adopts as what he openly calls "the perfection of man." To attain it, he says, is the "supreme good" for man, and whatever assists in the quest for it is his "true good" while what hinders that quest is evil.

We can see now that "the perfection of man" in this sense has direct relation to "perfection" in the sense of reality. For man's perfection is that state in which his power of action is greatest. That will be when he thinks most adequately, by the third kind of knowledge, and that again is when he sees all things as they are in God, *sub specie aeternitatis*, or when his ideas are as God's ideas and his mind encompasses as much of reality as possible and so achieves as high a degree of perfection as it can.

The various senses of "good" and "evil" which Spinoza criticizes, as well as those which he adopts, all fit consistently into his conception of the nature of reality. Imaginary goods are in general not real or true, and the terms as used in reference to them are merely ways of speaking. They mostly indicate what people commonly (but for the most part mistakenly) believe to be to their advantage. What really is to their advantage, however, is what enhances their power of action and may rightly be called good. Likewise, the usual sense of perfect, though it corresponds to nothing in nature but only to the general ideas we construct to aid our imagination, nevertheless bears a kind of approximate analogy to true perfection which is real completion and fulfilment; and there is a legitimate sense in which we can speak of the perfection of mankind and form an ideal of character which is the ultimate goal of our *conatus*.

From all this, however, it follows that evil is not real in any sense. We have seen that what is positively contained in our ideas of imagination is not error, and that their error consists only in what they leave out. So also with the passions, it is what they lack in understanding that makes them evil. It is the failure, the reduction in power, of action which makes them unpleasant, not anything positive. What we seek through desire is positive augmentation of power, increase in perfection. That is good only; our failure consists in falling short. So every desire is potentially good and what constitutes evil is only what it lacks. Our behavior is vicious only so far as we imagine, and imagination is a distorted, truncated version of the truth. So vice is a distorted and perverted effort towards the good. What is bad about it is not its positive content but is mere privation. So far as we think adequately we cannot act badly and so far as we think inadequately we simply fail to come up to the required standard. There are occasions when we do both at once, when we are affected through *imaginatio* by passion and at the same time think in certain respects adequately. Then passion may overcome and defeat the power of adequate thought. But here again the aspect of evil is just the failure to act in accordance with our reason and nothing *positive* in our actual deed. Evil, therefore, is nothing positive; it is only an incident or characteristic of a relatively low grade of perfection, or in simpler terms it is merely privation of good—a lower degree of advantage.

To support this argument further we should have to examine and analyze particular instances of evil, and we cannot profitably do that until we have further discussed the nature of virtue and vice. But we may glance at a few examples that Spinoza gives in his correspondence and see how he illustrates and explains his theory. The acts of Orestes and of Nero, he says, considered simply as positive acts and insofar only as what they were in themselves were exactly alike: they were matricide; but we do not consider them to be equally evil. Nero's act is evil because it is *un*-grateful, piti-*less*, *im*-pious, and *dis*-obedient—all merely negative terms. Orestes' act is less evil because it is a positive effort to expiate the murder of his father. To kill another person, even one's own mother, becomes evil only in the light of what it fails positively to achieve. In certain circumstances the act itself might even be regarded as virtuous (if, for instance, it was intended to save the victim from intolerable suffering). What Spinoza says is that so far as it "expresses essence" it is not evil, but only so far as it fails to do so. In like manner every action performed has some positive content which in itself, so Spinoza maintains, is not evil but has some degree of goodness (even if a low degree). Its badness is simply its failure to be better—a mere privation.

The view may be further explained and illustrated by considering, for example, Nero's action as the result of a desire to rid himself of certain obstructions to his own exercise of power. The desire purely in itself is not evil; but Nero's idea of the exercise of power was merely an idea of his imagination. As Plato taught us, real power is not the unfettered ability to do whatever you fancy, to kill your enemies (or those you imagine to be enemies) and benefit your imagined friends. True power is the exercise of reason, and in social and political relations it consists in the cooperation, the mutual trust, and devotion of men. The evil of Nero's act was incident upon his failure to understand this; in his imagination that power consisted in the unbridled indulgence of his passions, which resulted eventually only in revealing his own weakness and led to his downfall and death. In short, the evil consisted in failure and deprivation, not in any positive aspect of his behavior. If and so far as it expressed essence it was not evil.

Just as there is no error in God's intellect, so also there is no evil in God at all, because evil is mere privation, mere omission from the act or condition of what actually is in God. Evil, then, is purely relative. Absolute evil is sheer nonexistence, just as absolute perfection is absolute existence. The Devil, of necessity, does not exist. Yet there is a sense in which, because God is all-inclusive, he does contain every grade of imperfection, for he contains every grade of perfection, the lowest as well as the highest. But the imperfection of the lowest is simply its distance from the highest (what it lacks), and its whole reality is its positive content. It *is* a grade of perfection, if only a very low one. There can be nothing absolutely imperfect except what has no positive content whatsoever—that is to say, nothing—nonbeing itself.

One final clarification must be made before we pass to our next topic. Because Spinoza says that what men find pleasant they call good, and what they find unpleasant they call evil, and because in the 8th Proposition of Part IV of the *Ethics* he states that "the knowledge of good and evil is nothing other than the feeling of pleasure or pain so far as we are conscious of it," some commentators regard his theory as hedonism— that is, the doctrine that the good is nothing but pleasure and virtue simply the pursuit of pleasure as the ultimate end of all desire and action. This is another of the many misinterpretations and misunderstandings to which Spinoza's teachings are prone.

As we have already seen, he does not hold that all pleasant experiences are truly good. But the retort may come that hedonists do not hold that view either, for they say that the true good is the greatest and most unmixed pleasure, and some pleasant experiences are mixed with pain or have painful consequences, which thus disqualify them from being truly desirable. That, however, is not why Spinoza disqualifies them. It is because they only feel like but are not in fact transitions to greater perfection. The true end and aim of desire and the supreme good, for Spinoza, is not pleasure but the power of action. Transition to it is felt as pleasant but that is only incidental. It is impossible to aim at a transition except by aiming at the end towards which the transition is made. The supreme good for man is the augmentation of his activity (properly so called) by the perfection of his intellect. This is, indeed, always pleasant, but the pleasure is not the end at which action aims; it merely supervenes upon success, as Aristotle taught, "as the bloom of youth upon those in the flower of their age."

When Spinoza says that our knowledge of good and evil is nothing other than our consciousness of pleasure and pain, he is being quite consistent. For pleasure and pain are ideas (as are all affects, or feelings)—they are states of consciousness. Every idea involves an idea of itself for all consciousness is self-consciousness. Ideas are not, he insists, dumb pictures on a tablet. Thus our knowledge of any transition towards or away from greater perfection will be our awareness of pleasure and pain. But transition towards greater perfection is the true good and transition to lesser perfection is evil. Pleasure and pain, however, are affects and affects are, so far as they are passions, the results of external causes. The true good is what conduces to action, and that is conduct proceeding from our own nature alone. The fact that such conduct is pleasant does not imply an identity of pleasure with good. In fact, inasmuch as pleasure and pain are passions they both equally (though in different ways) fall short of the supreme good for man—pain obviously because it is transition away from that good, pleasure insofar as it is incident only upon lower levels of perfection, is concomitant with passivity, and is therefore at least in part illusory. Good and evil are only what we know *for certain* to be either to our true advantage or obstructive of the attainment of it; and we know for certain only if we think adequately, if we act freely or from our own nature alone.

12

Morality and the Good Life

Human Nature

CONTEMPORARY PHILOSOPHERS, AMONG them Jean-Paul Sartre, have denied that there is any such things as "human nature." There is no set structure to which human personality does or must conform, no common characteristic which all human beings share, no fixed essence with which humanity can be identified. The reason for this, it is said, is that human beings, as the subjects of consciousness and action, are free agents and each makes himself what he is and re-creates himself with every fresh choice freely taken. Despite appearances, Spinoza would in some sense and to some extent agree. For him the essence of a man is peculiar to himself, as is the essence of every finite mode, and there is no general characteristic common to all mankind such that we could designate it "humanity" or "human nature." When Spinoza speaks of "the essence of the human mind," or uses similar phrases, he is referring to the essence of each particular human being, and he denies emphatically that the general idea of man or humanity is anything but an aid to the imagination such as philosophers might excogitate but which corresponds to nothing real. Also, while he denies with equal emphasis the kind of indeterminate freedom of will that seems implied by modern Existentialism, we have seen that he does not deny freedom to men so far as they act autonomously; and in such acts they do determine themselves and make themselves what they are.

It is nevertheless true for Spinoza that a man is but a finite mode of Substance and what he is and does is largely (if not wholly) determined by

85

other finite modes. He is, like everything else, subject to the laws of nature. Certain modes of behavior are thus "natural" to him in the sense that they are what the laws of nature impose. Spinoza therefore says of men that they do certain sorts of things and are subject to certain kinds of influence (for example, the passions) "by nature."

> Everyone exists by the highest law (*jure*) of nature, and conse-
> quently everyone does by the highest natural right (*jure*) that
> which follows of necessity from his nature; and to that extent
> everyone judges, by the highest natural right, what is good, what is
> bad, and consults his own advantage by his own insight, defends
> himself, strives to protect what he loves and destroy what he hates.
> (*Ethics*, IV, xxxvii, S2)

By nature a man is a finite mode, and all finite modes strive to persist each in its own essence; but for that very reason the power of each to preserve itself is infinitely less than the powers of all the rest taken together. Within the face of the whole universe the existences and activities of all the finite modes are adapted one to another so that the total proportion of motion and rest is maintained constant. Thus the *conatus* of every finite mode is limited by that of every other, and though they may differ among themselves in their degrees of excellence, there is none so strong and powerful that no other can be found which does not surpass it in power, for bodies may combine to any extent and their diversity is infinite.

Man, therefore, cannot by any means bring it about that he should not be part of nature, or that he should not be subject to the impingement of outside causes, except those which can be understood through his own nature and of which he is the adequate cause. It is therefore impossible that he should not be subject to passion, for he must of necessity follow and obey the common order of nature and accommodate himself to it as the nature of things demands.

It follows that man is by nature an ambivalent creature. He is finite and struggles to exist against superior odds, subject to the effects of external causes beyond his control which generate in him inadequate ideas and subject him to passion. Yet also, the true essence of his mind is intelli-gence and through understanding he becomes the adequate cause of his own action. Such action is intelligible (Spinoza says) through his own nature (i.e., essence) alone, is thus autonomous and free. Consequently what a person does from passion he does by nature, and also when he acts autonomously it is specifically from his own essential nature as an intelligent being that he acts. He is by nature finite, yet the nature of his finite essence is to be a thinking, intelligent being capable of free action, and in both respects, both so far as he has inadequate and so far as he has adequate ideas, his power of continuing in his own being is the same *conatus* or striving. Whether he suffers or whether he acts he does so "by nature," and the more so from his own nature when he is self-determined. This duality in the nature of mankind is especially relevant to morality, the aim of which is to discover and realize the best way to live; and it has a special significance in Spinoza's theory of the state and social order, which is to be the subject of the next chapter.

Human Weakness

What is truly good for man is what increases his power of action; but so far as he is affected by passion he is under the sway of external causes, and the strength and persistence of the passion depends upon the strength of the external causes and not on that of the man's own *conatus*. What is nearer to us both in space and time (other things being equal) affects us more strongly than what is more remote, so that even when we know that our behavior is likely to have adverse consequences, if the immediate gains seem attractive, we pursue them in preference; and even when we know quite definitely that a seemingly pleasant object is really harmful to us, the mere knowledge cannot, by virtue simply of being true, remove the affect which impels us towards the object of our desire.

As we saw earlier, knowledge does not necessarily remove the illusion imposed upon us by *imaginatio*. Even when we know that the sun is millions of miles away, it still looks as if it were comparatively near, when we see it reflected in a pond, even though we know that it is in the sky, it still appears to be in the water. Likewise what we know to be to our detriment still appeals to us as pleasant, if the knowledge does not excite in us a stronger affect. And if the harm is only anticipated in the future, or is (in our view) contingent, or both, while the pleasant object is within our grasp, the desire for it will be stronger than any inclination to forego the pleasure. For similar reasons, *mutatis mutandis*, we shall avoid what appears to us unpleasant and flee what seems dangerous, even when we know that it would be in our best interests to suffer the pain or face up to the danger. The reason for this, Spinoza explains, is that a true idea, so far as it is true, does not remove what is positive in a false one. In fact, it confirms and supplements it. For what makes the idea false is simply its deficiency, what it lacks. So with passion, what in it is deceptive and bad is only its failure to increase our autonomy, and it fails to the extent that it is caused by external influences and to the extent that it is not under our own control—so far, in short, as our *conatus* is surpassed and over-whelmed by external causes. Our vices, therefore, are our proneness to give way to passion. When *imaginatio* is the level of our knowledge this happens all the time. But even when we know better we succumb to temptation: "The good that I would that I do not; but the evil that I would not that I do."

The Life of Reason

But this state of affairs is by no means inevitable. The *conatus* is involved in both vice and virtue, for we strive to persevere in our own being both so far as we have inadequate ideas and so far as our ideas are adequate. But virtue is the successful exercise of the urge to persist in our own being and so to increase our own power of action. This we do from adequate knowledge alone. In other words, virtue is rational action: to live, to do, and to preserve oneself as reason dictates. What we do by reason, Spinoza tells us, is nothing other than seek to understand, and so far as we use reason we judge only that to be of value to us which leads to the perfection of the intellect. He defines good as what we know for certain to be of value to us and that which we certainly know to prevent our obtaining it is bad. But we can know for certain only through adequate ideas. Only understanding, therefore, will be of ultimate value, for only by understanding (by reason) can we know for certain what is to our advantage. But, how, in the light of what has been said above, can this understanding be of any avail and how can we ever act virtuously? The answer to this question is of prime importance, but it must be postponed until we have considered what it is that reason prescribes. This will in some measure indicate how the question may be answered and will also discover to us the difference between the good life and the bad.

As our fundamental urge is to preserve and persevere in our own essence and thus to increase our power of action, it is obvious that reason can require nothing contrary to our nature. Its primary dictate is to know and be oneself. "Nobody tries to conserve his own being for the sake of anything else," writes Spinoza. Each person is an end in himself and is his own end. To say this will no doubt arouse immediate objection, for though, since Kant, we have been accustomed to admit that all humanity is an end in itself, is it not destructive of morality to maintain that each person is an end to herself or himself and the only end? Is it not arrant selfishness alone that would lead a man to try to conserve his own being for its own sake alone? If all virtue springs only from our efforts to preserve ourselves and increase our own power, can there be any motive other than selfishness?

The question is no new one in ethics, but it rests on a confusion between selfishness, as the name for a vice, and self-regard, which is an inevitable aspect of all deliberate action. All deliberate action is the result of choice. However selflessly I may act, if what I do is of any moral significance, I must have chosen to do it. But I cannot choose without preference, for what I do is chosen from alternatives. I must choose either to do it or to refrain from doing it, and whichever is chosen is what I prefer. But what I prefer I consider to be in some way of superior value or importance, and it must be of value and importance to me, or I could not prefer it. It is only if I rank another's benefit of greater importance *to me* than my own that I can act unselfishly. This element of preference and choice is essential to all deliberate action, and thus to all action of moral significance. Consequently all such action involves some degree of self-regard. It is to this inevitable aspect of action that Spinoza refers when he says that nobody strives to conserve his own being for the sake of anything else. All action is an expression of the will to live, and that, Spinoza contends, we can only lose if our *conatus* is completely overcome by external causes. Loss of the will to live, or the desire to destroy oneself can result only from madness or from the most abject despair, that is, only when one is utterly overwhelmed by passion.

On the other hand, the more rationally one pursues the means to persevere in one's own being, the more does one's action become unselfish and other-regarding at the same time. For Spinoza demonstrates that whatever agrees with our nature is of benefit to us and only what is contrary to our nature is harmful. Men, he says, do not agree in nature so far as they are subject to passion, because passion is the effect upon them of alien natures; and things agree only in positive respects, whereas a man suffers passion merely to the extent that his essence is negated. But so far as men act they agree, and in agreement they are more useful and beneficial to one another than anything else. It follows that a major dictate of reason is that we should strive, at the same time as we try to improve our own intellects, to improve those of others, and whatever we hold, by reason, to be of benefit to ourselves, we shall by the same token hold to be good for everybody. Thus we shall seek the good of others for the same reason and by the same means as we seek our own, and what we know to be the supreme good for ourselves we know to be equally the supreme good for everybody. This conclusion is made more obvious and more compelling when we realize that the perfection of the understanding requires its advance to the third kind of knowledge, which is the knowledge of all things mediated through an adequate idea of God's attributes. Accordingly, as our chief aim is to understand and to perfect our intelligence, our supreme objective must necessarily be the knowledge of God, through which alone all things can be adequately conceived. That this supreme objective cannot but be the same for all is thus manifestly and finally established as the ultimate dictate of reason.

But long before we get to this final goal, even at the level of *imaginatio* the need for mutual love and cooperation between people is borne in upon us. For the *conatus* is operative also in conjunction with inadequate thinking, and we have seen that we tend to have similar emotions to those of others similar to ourselves, and that we try to do what we imagine pleases others. But, apart from this, each one in isolation is at so great a disadvantage in his or her lone effort at self-preservation that each needs the help of others even to survive. It becomes apparent even to common opinion which falls short of reason that nothing is more useful and more helpful to mankind than man. This is the basis of all society, which rests as much upon instinct and affect as upon reason. Whereas need and natural desire promote mutual cooperation, however, passion engenders conflict between people as it does within the mind of each. But reason necessarily leads people to agree, for by reason each knows for certain what is good and sees that it is the same for all. Accordingly, Spinoza writes:

> Nothing more useful to man for the conservation of his being and the enjoyment of rational life is to be found than a man who is led by reason. Hence, because we know of nothing among particular things which is more excellent than a man who is led by reason, each one of us can show how accomplished he is in skill and ingenuity in no better way than by so educating men that they may finally come to live by their own rule of reason. (*Ethics*, IV, App. 9)

As humans are more versatile than other creatures, it is equally true that they are more dangerous to one another when they become victims of passions such as envy and hatred. But these passions do not serve to gain even their apparent ends. In such conflicts we cannot subdue men's minds simply by violence and strife, but much more by love and generosity, for we have observed that when love overcomes hatred it is, for that reason, all the stronger. Nevertheless, the majority of people are led by passion and not by reason, and although there is a solid foundation of social living, great skill and care are needed to maintain peace and harmony and to restrain the excesses of the violent. The principles upon which this is to be done with justice and right are for political philosophy to work out.

Virtue and Vice

Pleasure in itself and intrinsically is always good, but indirectly it may be a source of evil. Titillation, pleasure affecting only part of the body, can be excessive and bad so far as it involves pain and harm to other parts or at other times. We may say that if pleasure is ever bad it is because of its consequences or its concomitants, but is not so in itself. Pain, on the other hand, is always intrinsically bad, but it may in some circumstances be good, for instance as a deterrent from harmful pleasures, or a warning against greater evils. Cheerfulness, or exhilaration, can never be too great, it is always a good but it does not often arise and is usually overlaid by less healthy affects; melancholy is always to be deplored. Love and desire can become excessive and may lead to obsessions with money, sex, or advancement (ambition) which, Spinoza asserts, are as much diseases as are other forms of delirium and insanity. Hatred, related as it is to pain, is always bad both in itself and in its consequences, for it leads to various kinds of malevolence. Spinoza does not countenance even hatred of evil-doing in others. That is vindictive and harmful to both parties. Evil-doing is rather to be pitied for it is the source of unhappiness in the agent as much as, or even more than, in the victim, because it is the product of conflicting passions, or of some excessive obsession. The best response to wrong-doing is to return good for evil and love for hatred for reasons which have already been stated.

Pity, however, is an affect and indulged as such is mere sentiment. It is not a rational motive and may well be misplaced:

> . . . he who is easily touched with the emotion of pity and moved by the misery of others to tears, often does something of which he later repents; as much because we do nothing from affect which we certainly know to be good as because we are easily deceived by false tears. (*Ethics*, IV, l, S)

To feel no pity at all, however, for the misfortunes of others would be inhuman, and it has the beneficial effect of prompting a desire to help the victims of evil. But whatever may be done from affect (or imagination) can also be done through reason, so that the virtue of compassion proper is an action and not simply a passion and whatever feeling accompanies it is an active emotion.

Hope and fear are equally signs of weakness and are neither of them good in themselves, for they result from ignorance; and confidence, joy, despair, and disappointment are equally unprofitable, if not more so. Frequently they are based on false report and are seldom or never rationally appropriate, for the reasonable man knows that all things happen according to the laws of nature, whose workings are not appropriate objects for hope, fear, disappointment and the like, while despair (as will become progressively apparent) is always the product of excessive, conflicting, or perverted passion.

Overestimation and contempt, whether of others or of oneself, are always bad. Overestimation of oneself leads to pride which is a form of madness, in Spinoza's opinion; of others can make them proud and ourselves ambitious in our desire to please them. Self-love and excessive complacency, as well as being self-deceptive, is usually odious to others, and the follies of those who think too well of themselves, are boastful and vainglorious, arouse contrary emotions in others which almost inevitably lead to the downfall and humiliation of the proud.

Humility and repentance are not ranked as virtues by Spinoza, so far as they are merely passive affects. He concedes however that they may be beneficial so far as they restrain people from ill-doing, so they are commended in the Bible by the prophets and encouraged by moralists and legislators. They are good, in a qualified sense, as deterrents. But again whatever beneficial actions result from them could better be done from rational motives.

By contrast pride and self-subjection are both vicious. The proud love flatterers and hate those who tell them the truth about themselves. Both the proud and the abject are envious of others, especially any whose accomplishments they imagine to be superior to their own, and they depreciate their virtues either to aggrandize themselves or to find consolation for their own failings. They criticize in order to condemn rather than to remedy.

Though it is often necessary to restrain men from wrong-doing by fear, this is not good in itself and is evil in excess. In politics it makes men slaves rather than law-abiding citizens, and they will rebel when opportunity serves; in religion it leads to superstition and exploits human ignorance and weakness. It is, therefore, to be deplored and avoided, except so far as, in politics, this is impossible without detriment to the general welfare.

So much for the vices; we have not given an exhaustive account of them, but enough, perhaps, to illustrate the general principle that vice is the product of inadequate thinking and passion, which if they ever produce good conduct do so by accident or indirectly, inasmuch as by *imaginatio* we can never know for certain what is to our ultimate advantage.

The reasonable man, by contrast, does know for certain. He perceives things under the aspect of eternity and is not swayed by passion to prefer proximate pleasure to future good; thus he evaluates things and courses of action by invariant standards. He will find nothing to excite contempt, hate, or derision, nor will he be subject to sentimental pity. He will return love and generosity for hate and spitefulness, yet he will show gratitude for benevolence and the solicitude of others. He seeks good directly and does not act only through fear of greater evils. He avoids danger prudently and not from cowardice, and he faces danger when necessary to the performance of good actions, which he sees as his duty. These will be, as we have said, what lead to the improvement of his own and of others' understanding, and what are necessary to the common welfare of society. He will decline the favors of the ignorant, but with tact so as to give no offense. He will always act honorably, for to do otherwise would be self-contradictory. If it were virtuous to deceive others it would be reasonable to do so and would be equally reasonable for everybody. But universal deception is impossible, for it implies universal distrust and disbelief. One can deceive only those who believe, and betray only those who trust. Honor and truthfulness are thus the only rational possibility.

The reasonable man is no ascetic, though he is no libertine and does not indulge in such pleasures as are bad in excess.

> It is characteristic of the wise man, I say, to refresh himself with moderate and pleasant food and drink and to seek recreation in scents the amenities of green plants, adornments, music, games, theatre and other such entertainments as may be enjoyed by anybody without harm to others. (*Ethics*, IV, xlv, S)

So he will achieve an equable contentment and will be aware of his rationality as its source. This will give him a satisfaction with himself which is neither pride nor vainglory, but self-respect, and an inner peace which is the most desirable state of mind. It is not to be found in the pursuit of any other end save that of reason.

Such a man is free in precisely the sense that Spinoza admits. He is free from passion and therefore from compulsion by external causes. His acts of mind are determined only by his intellect, which is the true essence of his mind; his ideas are adequate, and so his mind is self-determined. His body, as the counterpart of his intellect, is clearly conceived in its relations to other bodies and acts appropriately to this understanding of its place in nature. As nature determines him so he determines himself. But he remains finite and so can never be fully self-determinate and free, and is always to some degree subject to passion. The question remains how he can ever become free to any extent, for being finite, how can he ever escape the compulsion of outside causes?

The Power of the Intellect

As the first step towards an answer to the last question, we may remind ourselves that the human body, finite as it is, is more "excellent" in its structure and functioning than bodies lower in the scale of complexity and can accomplish far more on its own than others by domesticating, so to speak, and including in its own economy, the outside causes upon which other bodies depend for movement and self-conservation. Its mind, in consequence, is correspondingly more able to understand. Its degree of finiteness is less, and of perfection more, than those of inferior bodies and their ideas. But more important still, the ideas of the human body are its consciousness of itself and are all of them self-illuminating. There is of each of them an idea of itself; so its mind is self-conscious and self-reflective. By reflection upon its passions and its inadequate ideas it can, therefore, go beyond *imaginatio* to the levels of *ratio* and *scientia intuitiva*. Through its adequate knowledge, and especially through the third and highest kind, the human mind can overcome and subdue its passions, and can convert them into action.

As soon as we form a clear and distinct idea of an affect it ceases to be a passion. The more we can understand affects, therefore, and form adequate ideas of them, of our own bodies and what causes effect in them, the less subject are we to passions. And there is no affect with respect to which we cannot do this, at least to some extent. In understanding our affects we form new ideas of them, adequate ideas, of which the ideas of their causes are not the cause. For instance, suppose that I hate another person because I imagine him as the cause of pain I have suffered as a result of what he has said about me; if I come to see that my pain and annoyance is really the result of my own vanity, or of his misunderstanding, or even of frailty or stupidity on his part, my feeling towards him changes. In general it is true that as soon as we understand the emotions of ourselves and others and how they are caused, our more violent reactions tend to abate or at least to change. This is one of the underlying principles of the technique of modern psychoanalysis, which seeks to make a subject aware of the hidden causes of his emotions, making them change and dissipate as he becomes aware of their source.

Any desire which springs from an inadequate idea is liable to be vicious. But the same desire arising out of an adequate idea is virtuous. Thus a desire to help the poor arising from mere sentiment may do more harm than good; whereas the same desire, prompted by an understanding of people's real needs and those of social order, will result in much more beneficial action. By forming adequate ideas of our desires, therefore, we can convert them from passions to actions.

Things conceived as necessary excite less emotion than when they are thought to be contingent, and such emotion as they do arouse is much more in our power. But reason conceives all things as necessary and so views them all with equanimity. Also it sees events as the effects of diverse causes, not of one only, and this tends to reduce the intensity of the emotions felt towards those causes severally. At the same time an emotion produced by numerous causes is more stable and less fickle than one caused by a single thing. So, here again, reason enables us to modify and overcome passion.

Finally, the third kind of knowledge relates all things to God and likewise all the affections of the body so far as they are clearly and distinctly (adequately) conceived. But Spinoza has earlier established that the mind's contemplation of its own power of action is a source of pleasure, and this adequate knowledge of its body and its affections is active, as has been explained, and is the exercise of that power, which is now seen as caused by God; and so the mind's enjoyment becomes love for God. With the increase of intuitive knowledge of the third kind, this love of God occupies the mind to the exclusion of all else, and as everything is referred to him as cause, it envelopes and supersedes all the affects. It is, *par excellence* an active emotion and not a passion and is, of necessity, the most harmonious state of mind.

When all things are understood adequately in this way, we recognize the mere negativity of all evil and cease to be affected by it with pain and sorrow. God is seen as the cause of this deliverance also, and our love for him is further confirmed. So we are brought to a consideration of the nature of religion and its significance in man's life. But for that we have reserved a later chapter, and we must turn first to those matters arising out of the foregoing discussion, which concern society and the state.

13

Politics

The Two-Tier Nature of Mankind

MEN NEED FOR their survival many things that each is unable to provide by his own unaided efforts. Their interdependence is therefore obvious and has been noted by Spinoza in the *Ethics*. There too he has demonstrated the dual nature of man as a finite entity, and how, under the impulse universal to all things each to persist in its own being, man commonly seeks what he finds attractive, avoids what is painful, loves and cherishes the former, hates and seeks to destroy the latter under the influence of passion, and, for the most part, does so unsuccessfully. Yet impelled by that same *conatus* to increase his own power of action, he can through the self-reflective character of his consciousness come to think adequately and to act rationally; and when he does that he understands clearly wherein his true good lies and recognizes that it is common to all persons. This conclusion is reinforced by his realization of his own dependence upon others and theirs upon him and his rational understanding that nothing is more useful to him than his fellow beings, even when they are subject to passion. For nobody can live in complete isolation, and, although hatred and envy drive people apart and, being more versatile and cunning than other beasts they can be mutually more dangerous, in the main love overcomes hatred because it is the more positive, more unmixed, and thus the stronger passion. When led by the dictates of reason, however, persons are without qualification, more valuable to one another than anything else can be, so that the dictate of reason is to seek peace and concord and the lasting friendship of reasonable people.

Here then we have the rational foundation of social life, and on this basis Spinoza constructs his theory of the state and civil society. We shall understand it clearly only if we bear in mind the twofold character of human beings, both phases of which are always present as aspects of their behavior. They are never totally devoid of intelligence (apart from extreme cases of mental deficiency), nor are they ever completely rational—for nothing can prevent their being finite parts of nature or augment their power of action to such a degree as completely to overwhelm all opposing forces. In the sphere of politics the primary fact to be faced is that "men are led more by blind desire than by reason" (*TP*, II, 5), a fact which must be counteracted if they are to be able to live together and minister to one another's needs as is essential for their survival. This is a minimum requirement of reason. In social life, therefore, reason is operative from the outset, but its first task is to counteract, and so far as possible to restrain, the irrational and passionate conduct that is prevalent among the majority of people. How this is to be done without either suppressing their potentialities and making them slaves, or giving undue rein to their desires so as to endanger social solidarity, is what political theory has to reveal.

Natural Law

Thinkers of the seventeenth century inherited the conception of natural law from those of the middle ages, who in turn received it from the Roman lawyers and the Stoics. It was not understood to mean what we understand by "law of nature" today. It was not conceived as a system of observed regularities ordering events in nature, although that idea was not excluded from it. Natural law was held to be a prescription of reason imposed upon human conduct and inherent in the nature of things. Alternatively, it was regarded as the law imposed by God upon both nature and man; or, again, it could be both, for reason was considered (at any rate by such thinkers as Anselm and Aquinas) as one form of revelation, so that at least an important part of God's law was discovered to us by reason.

The seventeenth-century philosophers took over the idea of a law inherent in the nature of the world and also in human nature, which dictated rules of behavior to man anterior to any civil society. So they imagined a condition of men prior to the formation of a civilized order which they called the state of nature, in which human behavior and the relations between men were governed by natural law.

These notions were used to give a philosophical account and justification of the authority of the sovereign power in a politically organized society over its subject people. The call for such justification was felt with the rise of a spirit of individual freedom awakened by the Reformation; for the great reformers, Luther, Melanchthon, and Calvin had challenged the age-old authority of the Roman Church and set up in its place (at least, in the first instance) the authority of individual conscience. If this challenge could appeal and succeed as impressively as it did, a similar challenge to the authority of the state was a natural consequence. In the sixteenth and seventeenth centuries treatises appeared on the nature and origin of political organization, on one side giving theoretical grounds for the condemnation of tyranny and justification for rebellion against it, on the other, doing the same thing for the supremacy of the state as a secular authority regulating the conduct of its members and prescribing the form of their relations to one another.

For both of these purposes, appeal was made to natural law and a state of nature in which there was no organized society, but in which men were subject to natural law alone. This natural state was supposed to precede the civil state and was conceived by some as a condition of complete anarchy, in which men, each following his own desires and passions, were in perpetual conflict, and by others as a quasi-social condition in which a code of natural law was obeyed. In both cases man was held to follow the law of nature—of his own nature in particular as a feature of nature in general—and, according as the particular philosopher regarded human nature to be quarrelsome or amiable, so he conceived the state of nature as chaotic or as relatively peaceful. There was, however, general agreement that the state of nature involved the singular disadvantage that each man must be his own judge in disputes and the executor of his own remedies without recourse to impartial arbiters who might dispense a modicum of justice.

Some device had to be found, therefore, for converting the state of nature into the civil state, and this was done by postulating an original contract between individual men, or between a group of men and one (or a few) selected to bear authority, or both, by which the individuals surrendered their natural rights (that is, their rights under natural law) to a supreme political power authorized to make, promulgate, and administer a civil law. In some versions the contract laid down conditions limiting the scope of the sovereign authority in specific ways; in others reasons were shown why no such limitation was either possible or desirable.

The most celebrated proponents of doctrines of this kind were Jean Bodin, Althusius, DuPlessis-Mornay, John Locke, Hugo de Groot

(Grotius), and Thomas Hobbes, whose works (undoubtedly those of the last two, if no others) were probably known to Spinoza. Spinoza, however, adapted the conceptions of natural law and natural right to his own metaphysical system and the idea of human nature which followed from it as I have explained. In his theory of society and the state, however, although he makes some reference to an original contract in his theological-political treatise, in his later writing the fictitious description of a state of nature falls away, and in his more mature work (the *Tractatus Politicus*) he dispenses with the contract altogether.

For Spinoza, natural law is the law of God, for God and Nature are one and the same. Man's nature is part of this; he is a finite mode of Substance of a specific degree of "excellence" or perfection. What man does by nature, therefore, he does according to natural law, and so, in Spinoza's words, by the highest natural right. By nature, we have already seen, each man desires whatever he imagines or conceives to be profitable to him and strives as much as he can to obtain it. This, therefore, he does by the highest right of nature; as he seeks to defend himself against attack and those he loves against harm, while he assails what he hates, and pursues whatever he enjoys. In short, whatever a man is able to do by nature he has a natural right to do and "natural rights," for Spinoza, are the same as natural powers or capacities.

In this view, he differs from almost every other political theorist except Hobbes; for most political philosophers who use the notion of natural right at all, make it the standard for civil right. They claim it as something to be preserved and defended against encroachment, whether by individuals or by public authority. In this form it was written into the constitutions of the United States and of revolutionary France; but Spinoza argues (and with considerable cogency) that Nature is not, and does not constitute, "a state within a state," but, apart from the civil condition with its properly constituted sovereign authority, man's natural right is virtually nil and is largely a sort of legal fiction, or, as he puts it, "an opinion." This indeed would follow logically from equating natural right with natural power. For, as we have discovered, the actual power of a single person is infinitesimal as compared with and pitted against that of the multitude of opposing forces. We can easily see how this is so.

The vast majority of men are led by blind desire and not by reason, and under the influence of passion are contrary in nature to one another. At the same time, as they are the most resourceful and cunning among animals they can be more dangerous to one another than anything else on earth. Moreover, as they are for the most part subject to envy, anger, and hatred, passions which drive them into conflict, "men are by nature enemies." If each, therefore, depended on his own power alone for his safety and preservation, his survival would be in the utmost jeopardy; his natural right (or power) would avail him little and, as Spinoza says, would be virtually nothing.

But by nature also man is rational and he is rational so far as he acts through his own intelligent nature alone. His real power is then at its maximum. But reason leads him to realize that the true good for man is common to all, that love is stronger than hatred and overcomes it, and that by mutual cooperation men can achieve far more than by strife and have much more power. So Spinoza declares that if all men *were* led by reason, each would be able to exercise his natural rights without injury to others. This, however, is seldom the case; in fact, if we expect the multitude to act reasonably we are wholly unrealistic and "dream of a golden age or of a fairy-tale." Accordingly, if men are to survive at all, they must combine their forces and live under a common power, a fact of which they must be aware whether they are moved by reason or passion; because all desire is for survival and for the enhancement of power, and it is too obvious to be missed that individuals in isolation can ensure neither. Natural (or any sort of) rights, therefore, can be enjoyed only in concert, but then the individual enjoys whatever rights he has only by the common will of the whole group.

In his earlier treatise (*Theologico-Politicus*), Spinoza contends that this original combining of individual powers implies an agreement between individuals, tacit but understood, to give up their natural rights to a common supreme authority; and as passionate men are fickle and few are to be trusted to keep agreements, nor will any do so unless he thinks it to be in his interests, the likelihood is that any such agreement will be broken whenever anybody believes it would be more advantageous to him to break it. The contract, therefore, if it is to be at all effective, must be enforced on individuals by the common power that it sets up.

No doubt this was written when Spinoza was most strongly under the influence of Hobbes. But he saw immediately that the argument contained the seeds of its own destruction, for if the common power depends upon people's keeping their agreement to give up their natural rights to the civil authority, that authority will inevitably lack power to enforce the agreement if the contract is broken. So even in the earlier political treatise he bolsters the argument by saying that nobody can doubt how much better it is to live under law and the direction of rational rules devised to insure true human welfare, than for everyone to do whatever he pleases, for everybody wishes to live securely and free from fear, which would be impossible if anger and hatred were more respected than reason. Taken together with the previous argument it then becomes apparent that there is no need for any contract, because if people will keep agreements only as long as it is in their interests to do so, and if they cannot doubt that it is more to their advantage to live under law than under the insecure and uncertain sway of passion, they already have a motive strong enough to subject themselves to authority without any fiction of an implicit contract.

Not surprisingly, then, we find no mention of a contract in the later *Tractatus Politicus*, where Spinoza tells us straightforwardly that apart from a common law, men's natural rights exist only in theory and amount to nothing in fact; for only in combination and by concurrence can they appropriate goods and lands they can cultivate and keep safe from attack. Thus, for man, the natural state really is the civil state, in which alone his natural rights or powers can be realized, and without which they are of no avail. In Spinoza's words:

> When men have common laws and all are led as if by one mind, it is certain that each has less power as the rest are more powerful; that is, he has in truth no right by nature except what the common law concedes to him.

Other writers assume a state of nature in which there are natural moral laws that all men are obliged to keep. But this Spinoza denies. He contends that in the natural state, as men's "rights" are their powers, anything is permissible and nobody is forbidden to do whatever he wishes. Hence there can be no wrong-doing in the presumed natural state, nor can there be any justice or injustice; for only in the civil state is there any right of property on the basis of which meaning can be given to the notion of justice. Strictly, therefore, morality exists only in a civil condition under some form of instituted government, and is founded in social custom and law. Commonly, Spinoza admits, we speak of morality as obedience to the law of reason and immorality as what violates rational precepts; but then it is only in an organized society governed by law that a life of reason can, in practice, be followed. Moreover, as we have already seen, the first precept of reason is to combine the powers of individuals into a common power which can defend them from one another as well as from alien predators. Further, he maintains, if men are not led by reason at all, it is scarcely conceivable that they could make common cause or live together in peace and with any degree of harmony.

Sovereignty

The corporate right and conjoint force of a united and organized people is the right and power of sovereignty, which may be vested in one man, in a select body of men or in the multitude is a whole. Rule by one man is monarchy, by a select few is aristocracy, and by all is democracy; but whichever is the case, authority must be so vested by common consent, for so far as the sovereign power acts in such a way as to lose the common support of the people, so far it will lose power to enforce the law. This is the sole limitation upon its power and authority, for no individual has strength enough to defy it single-handed, as it has greater power the more persons are combined in its support, and whatever it has power to do, it does by right. Consequently, it is the state which will decide what is right and good for the community, and not the individual; and it is the state alone that can enforce its decision. Nevertheless, this supreme and unchallengeable power depends upon and can be maintained only with the concerted support and consent of the mass of its subjects, and if any government does what a large number of its citizens deplore it will lose power accordingly to enforce its will. But no individual may or can be his own judge or act according to his own wishes alone without consideration of those of his fellow citizens, for if he did he would forfeit their cooperation, on which he depends for the amenities of life, and would, so far as in him lies, disrupt the social order which is the condition of peace and safety for all. The reasonable man, therefore, will, in Spinoza's view, obey the law, even though at times it seems, in his judgement, to enjoin what is unreasonable. For reason dictates that one should at all times prefer the lesser evil to the greater.

Consequently, the sovereign authority of the state is supreme in all matters except those over which it has no means to exercise its power; it is supreme even in matters of religion, for it has superior power and cannot effectively be opposed by individuals. It alone can make and enforce laws, wage war, negotiate treaties, punish wrongdoers (i.e., law breakers). It is not, however, subject to any law, not even its own, for the law is whatever the sovereign does or decides. It is "subject" to the law of nature, only in the inevitable sense that its right is limited by its power; and it is subject to the law of reason in the sense that this power will necessarily be reduced if it does anything which will alienate the support of the bulk of its citizens, nullify their fear of its power, or destroy their respect for its laws.

On the other hand, private opinions and beliefs are beyond the power of the civil authority, because these cannot be changed by force, and any attempt to enforce them is liable to disrupt the social order, because people resent most being treated as criminals on account of what they hold to be true, and will resist persecution. Moreover, they are generally admired for their resistance and for the strength of mind to adhere to their beliefs in face of danger to their persons. Spinoza therefore strongly advocates toleration of religious belief and expression, suppression of which, he says, only creates dissension and brings the government into disrepute and ridicule for treating upright men as criminals. It follows that the more a government is led by reason the greater will be its power and authority; and the more fully it has the support, the respect, and the approval of its subjects the less will its authority be assailable.

The conclusion to which this argument points is that whatever form of government a state may have, its power, in principle, is that of the whole people and rests with the community. A people that lives under a government established by common consent is what Spinoza calls a "free multitude," and when this is reflected in its institutions we have a democracy which is, in his view, the best form of state; because, in this sort of regime, the government must continually consult the people and can act only by common consent. So the laws will not be made in the interests of the lawgivers only, but in those of the whole body politic, and people will not be kept in subjection by sheer force, like slaves, but will, in obeying the law, be obeying their own will.

This is the doctrine stated in the *Tractatus Theologico-Politicus* (Ch. XVI) and it is remarkably advanced for its time, because it maintains a theory of sovereignty which is both absolute in its power and yet popular in its origin and appeal. Thus Spinoza anticipates Rousseau and political thinkers of at least a century later, who succeeded in reconciling the opposing theories of absolute sovereignty, as propounded by such thinkers as Bodin and Hobbes, and those of limited government, the prototypes of Liberalism, represented by Althusius and Locke. For Spinoza the two doctrines coalesce in his conception of reason as ultimately supreme, for what in the last resort gives absolute authority to the state is the power which depends upon the loyalty, unity, and concurrence of its people, "led as if by one mind"; but this can be fully achieved only so far as it acts rationally and aims at that common good which reason shows to be universal to all. The absolute will of the sovereign, therefore, is not ultimately different from the individual will, understood as the *conatus* to increase its power of action. The ideal end of both is the same; and a free people, obeying the law of the state willingly, because they see it as right and not simply for fear of penalties, is a nation the government of which consults the common welfare and expresses the common will. It is upon this condition that the absoluteness of both its power and its authority in principle depend.

To believe that the multitude, or men perplexed by public business, can be induced to live solely by the prescriptions of reason, is, however, to dream of a golden age; for men are more led by blind desire. One can approach the ideal, therefore, only by devising checks and balances which will restrain men's passions by providing counter advantages to greed and selfishness. Spinoza, therefore, does not attempt to construct an ideal state, or Utopia, but outlines political constitutions for monarchies, aristocracies, and democracies (the last he did not live to complete) which are so devised as to ensure a balance of interests among the classes and institutions of the state.

Peace and War between States

In interstate relations, however, the state of nature prevails—that is to say, there is no supreme authority, and each state consults only its own interests and acts within the limits of its own power. The sovereign power alone in any state can make treaties and alliances with other states, which it will do in accordance with its national interests. It will keep such treaties and remain loyal to such alliances only as long as those interests are served, or (what is the same) as long as no greater force than it can muster threatens reprisals if pacts are broken. If interest demands and power is sufficient, the state will wage war and make peace as it sees fit, for in interstate affairs, as in internal, the sovereign is its own arbiter and is subject to no higher authority.

Here again we see a difference of approach from those who held that in the state of nature a law of nature prevails, imposing natural rights and duties. Grotius, who took this view, maintained that states in their mutual dealings were subject to a code of laws which he set out in some detail under the title *De Jure Pacis et Belli* (Concerning the Law of Peace and War), to become the father of international law. But Spinoza, like Hobbes, saw that a law set out by theorists which was not and could not be enforced by any authority (there being no authority with sufficient power to compel states to conform) would be a law in name only, and that states would continue to act in their own interests alone, without regard to any alleged legal principles. In this he was right and his description of international relations remains accurate to this day, in spite of the development of elaborate codes of international law and institutions such as the United Nations, which are quite ineffectual in restraining powerful states and to which appeal is made only when interests are served or power is lacking to resort to force. It is for this reason that both Spinoza and Hobbes maintain that the natural relation between states is one of war, potential if not actual, even when temporarily nullified by insecure alliances. A significant example of this general truth occurred in Spinoza's lifetime, when in 1672 Charles II of England, having concluded a treaty of alliance with Holland, promptly joined forces with her enemy, Louis XIV of France, in a war of aggression against the Netherlands.

Political Freedom

The upshot of this doctrine as a whole is that political freedom consists not in license, nor in restraint of interference by the public power with individual rights, but in good government by a sovereign body which represents the whole people and regularly consults their wishes, which acts in the common interest and is tolerant of private opinions and expression (as long as the latter is not disruptive of public peace and order), which acts so as to retain the loyalty and cooperation of its citizens and is sufficiently powerful to keep foreign enemies at bay. For all his advocacy of tolerance, Spinoza does not favor violent revolution, because he believes that violence breeds only counterviolence, solves no problems, destroys the conditions of decent living and is more liable to promote than to abolish tyranny. But he is equally no advocate of tyranny, subjection, or repression, and sees political freedom as the self-determination of a nation of willingly cooperating citizens, loyally obeying the law of a government they can accept as acting in their own best interests. Just as individual freedom is autonomous action and the man who follows reason is most his own master, so the well-governed state is the freest and in it the individual can find the conditions which make possible a life according to reason. In fact, only in a well-organized social structure is it possible properly to follow the precepts of reason in private conduct, for unless the wilder human passions are forcibly restrained by a legally constituted sovereign power, the best efforts of the most reasonable individual to live an orderly and peaceful life with his fellows is liable to meet with scanty success.

14

Reason and Revelation

THE TRUTH ABOUT God and mankind is acquired through the perfection of the intellect, and the more we know of particular things, Spinoza tells us, the more we know of God. The perfection of the intellect, moreover, is the essence of God actualizing itself in and through one of its modes of thought, the human mind. According to Spinoza, the whole is immanent in every one of its parts, but in varying degrees of perfection. This is what he means by saying that Substance is the immanent cause of all things. Both in extension and in thought the modes vary in complexity and form a scale of increasing degrees of reality or completeness (perfection), and the human body is one of the most complex of finite modes, being capable of doing and suffering many things together, so that its mind is able to perceive many things. Further, we have been told that the more self-dependent the body is for its self-preservation, the greater is its mind's capacity for clear understanding. The human mind, however, is no less than an idea (of the human body) in the intellect of God, and to the extent that it is freed from confusion and passion, to that extent is it identical with at least a part of the divine intellect. The human *conatus*, the endeavor to persist in one's own essence, is the effort to realize that essence, which, we have seen, is the intellect, the persistence, or realization of which is its activity of adequate thinking. Further, Spinoza has shown that the *conatus* is the power of God at work in the finite mode. It is the immanent causality of God in operation.

In other contexts, Spinoza calls this inner working of the divine power the Holy Spirit; thus the perfection of the intellect in human beings is their becoming aware of the divine nature and its immanence in all things (including themselves), through the working in them of the Holy Spirit. "The highest good of the mind is the knowledge of God," writes Spinoza in Part IV of the *Ethics*, "and the highest virtue of the mind is to know God." So philosophy and religion coincide. The perfection of knowledge culminates in the knowledge of God, and that knowledge, being pure activity, is always pleasant. It is this at which the *conatus* aims and which is the highest object of desire. As pleasure combined with the idea of its cause is love, the knowledge of God is at the same time the love of God: that intellectual love of an infinite object which nothing can corrupt or surpass. The third kind of knowledge, therefore, *scientia intuitiva*, or intuitive science, in its consummation, is the revelation of God. It is indeed religion, for Spinoza declares: "Whatever we desire and do, of which we are the cause so far as we have an idea of God, or so far as we know God, I refer to as religion."

The intellectual love of God is unlike the common profane love between human individuals so far as that is a passion; because the intellectual love of God is wholly active. It is a love which does not and cannot seek any return, as does the passionate love of men and women. It is not subject to jealousy, or envy, nor is it corruptible by any overindulgence. It can never be felt to excess, and it contains no element of pain or evil. It tends, in the nature of the case, to fill the mind to the exclusion of all other desires and aims, or, more accurately, it is itself the fulfilment and achievement of all other desires and aims once they are fully understood; for it is the concomitant of that complete and adequate knowledge, in the light of which all desires are seen in proper perspective, their causes identified, and their ends properly valued. The objects ordinarily pursued in life are usually seen only through the medium of imagination, but by the third kind of knowledge (*scientia intuitiva*) they are seen in their true place in the whole, through that knowledge of the relevant attribute of God which absorbs and transcends all objectives and fills the mind with inexhaustible love and joy. This intellectual love of God is one and the same as God's love for himself, which is also, and includes, his love for humankind and all creation.

But the attainment of this philosophical goal, the highest achievement of reason, is an extremely arduous task, which few ever succeed in accomplishing. As Spinoza confesses, the way to it, although it can be discovered, is obviously very difficult, for so few ever find it, a fact that would be incredible if salvation were easily at hand and could be acquired without great labor. Who, indeed, would ignore or neglect it if it could be had without effort? The philosophical demonstrations that lead to it are beyond the comprehension of the multitude, and the task of mastering them can be undertaken by very few. Human beings are but finite creatures, and the vast majority are overwhelmed by the multiple effects of outside causes. They are for the most part a prey to passion and, as we have been told, are swept hither and yon like the waves of the sea blown by contrary winds. Only very few ever manage to rise above this welter of passion and vice.

If this were all that could be said, salvation would be unattainable by the greater part of mankind. But it is not the whole story. There is, according to Spinoza, another form of revelation leading to salvation by a different yet closely related route, and one available to any who will heed it. Not only through reason, but also through the imagination, God may in some sense be revealed, by means of prophecy, which exhorts us to live the sort of life that brings redemption from passion and sin. It is not a revelation of truth in its intellectual purity, but one which nevertheless can have similar moral consequences, and so can bring to those who embrace it divine contentment—that peace that the world (of carnal and mercenary desire) can never give.

At first it may seem surprising to claim that the divine nature can be revealed through the imagination, for have we not been shown that imagination is the source, and the sole source, of all error? Spinoza, however, does not say that imagination is necessarily always in error, rather the contrary; the error arises only with the judgement or affirmation made concerning its significance. His explanation of how revelation is possible through prophecy is not, therefore, inconsistent with his main doctrine, because he admits that prophecy does not reveal the truth in its clear and distinct explicitness; it is not science, nor are prophets scientists or philosophers. Prophecy is adapted in form, in style, and in content both to the character and circumstances of the prophet and to the beliefs and the intellectual capacity of his audience. The gift of prophecy is a special talent, like the gift of poetry or music. It is a kind of genius, which is psychologically inexplicable, but which is able, through imagery, parable, and allegory, to convey to its hearers what may legitimately be called the will of God.

As God is the cause of all things, he is likewise the cause of the gift of prophecy, and it is no error to say that God reveals himself and his law to the prophet in visions or by signs. The law of God so revealed is the moral law, that one should love God and one's neighbor, and should act justly and mercifully. That this is true virtue, is in itself the best and most advantageous way to live for all concerned, requiring no further reward or compensation, Spinoza has already demonstrated by rational argument. Those who cannot follow the reasoning may, nevertheless, be led

to embrace its conclusions through faith inspired by imaginative rep-
resentations of God as the supreme ruler of the world, imposing on
mankind a law of morality and exercising justice and mercy in the
judgement of his people. The blessedness of righteousness is its own
inherent character. The virtuous life is itself the good life and requires
nothing further to perfect it. But ordinary people, prone to passion, are
not usually inclined to virtue, and if they are incapable of the intellectual
development Spinoza prescribes, they can be led to a life of virtue only by
the belief that the special grace of God bestows salvation upon those who
live in peace and charity with their neighbors. This creed may be revealed
in figurative form, through signs and visions, which prophets interpret to
the relatively ignorant. Prophecy is the gift of such vision and interpretation, a gift that some specially endowed and exemplarily pious persons
inexplicably possess.

Not all visions are genuine, however, and not all prophets are true
prophets. How then are the true to be distinguished from the false? It is
not by signs and wonders: these do not identify the genuine prophets, for
even the Bible itself tells us that false prophets can simulate them.
Moreover, Spinoza insists that nothing could be learned from miracles,
even if any occurred. For miracles appeal only to ignorance of natural
law, which is God's law, and so can reveal nothing of God's nature. The
authenticity of the prophet depends solely on his message. If what he
teaches is what Spinoza identifies as the true and universal religion, he is a
true prophet; otherwise he is not. The true and universal religion is what
has already been identified by rational deduction as true virtue: tolerance,
charity, justice, and the love of God and one's neighbor.

The true prophet teaches that these precepts are the law of God and
that obedience to them leads to salvation. It is a law written in people's
hearts and not imposed from without; thus it is equally the law of their
own (their best) nature. The genuine devotee will obey it, therefore, for
its own sake and will find that it is its own reward. Nothing more is
needed—no special observances, no ritual, no belief in "sacred histories,"
no celebration of miraculous events—none of these is essential for salvation. On the other hand, those who practise the true religion are saved, be
they Jews, or Christians, Mohammedans, or pagans, for to have this
divine law in one's heart is itself to be inspired by the Holy Spirit.

The Hebrew prophets, Spinoza maintains, were not philosophers, nor
were they learned persons. Most of them shared the beliefs and superstitions of their age and wrote, or preached, under their influence. Also they
suited their style and language to the beliefs and understanding of the

people. None of this affects, or derogates from their message, however, the kernel of which is a moral teaching that is universally sound and in agreement with what reason requires.

Among the true prophets Spinoza gives a special place to Jesus, who not only taught the true and universal religion, but revealed the spirit of God directly in his own person and conduct without the aid of visions or special signs. So far Spinoza goes along with Christian doctrine, but he totally rejects belief in miracles as supernatural wonders. That the disciples believed in them and sincerely thought them to be evidence of Christ's divinity he had no doubt. But, he says, it would be no detriment to their teaching to hold that their belief in the miraculous was mistaken. As to what the churches have added in later times, most of this he finds unintelligible and ridiculous. Much, if not all, of these accretions he regards as mere superstition, a major source of wickedness, which corrupts the true faith and turns it into error.

Spinoza makes a clear distinction between true religion (*religio vera*) and superstition (*religio vana*). The latter is the product of fear and insecurity in adversity, which tosses its victims from one extreme of hope to the other extreme of fear, so that they resort to all kinds of fantastic beliefs in search of some assurance and consolation. This is the result of passion and its product is vice. Emotion and imagination lead people to think themselves subject to evil and fearsome spirits. They endue God with the attributes of passionate men and see him as a vengeful and jealous ruler visiting fearful retribution on those who displease him and rewarding those who placate his anger by offering him the objects of their own greed. They view any extraordinary meteorological or astronomical phenomenon as a sign of coming disaster, and give credence to tales of magical feats and miraculous events. Such beliefs, again, persuade them to the practice of outlandish ritual observances aimed at appeasing angry gods and inducing nature to behave in a favorable way. All of this is simply the fruit of ignorance and fear.

Miracles, as recorded in the Bible, Spinoza admits as events that actually happened, but he maintains that they were either natural events amenable to natural explanation, like Noah's rainbow, or events that we cannot explain because of our ignorance of natural laws, but which we could explain naturally if we knew more. Otherwise, they are imaginary tales told and believed by superstitious writers, or natural events misunderstood and misdescribed in all good faith by ignorant and superstitious people. The laws of nature are the laws of God (and vice versa), and without self-contradiction God neither could nor would act in contravention of them. The very idea of a miracle is therefore contradictory. Whatever account is given of the allegedly miraculous is of necessity an appeal to our ignorance, for by definition a miracle is an event that we cannot explain by natural laws. Miracles, therefore, can teach us nothing about the divine nature and cannot be evidence of divine origin, whether of the supposed miraculous event or of the teaching of a prophet which it is believed to validate.

Accordingly, superstition is not to be confused with religion, but equally the sort of revelation that comes through the imagination of the prophets is not to be identified as superstition, for true prophecy goes with outstanding virtue and with special genius, the evidence of which is the moral quality of the teaching and its agreement with the conclusions of sound reason.

All the same, it would seem that true blessedness is only fully attained with complete understanding, the clear and distinct comprehension of the nature of God and of the relation to him of everything else. It is this comprehensive insight alone that generates the intellectual love of God, that supreme wisdom and spiritual satisfaction in which all conceivable endeavor eventually fulfils itself. The synoptic view of all time and all reality under the form of eternity (combining Plato's and Spinoza's phrases) is the knowledge of things identical with God's own idea of himself, the acquisition of which by human creatures is their atonement with God.

Such insight and actively joyous satisfaction is eternal and transcends the merely psychical, the stream of consciousness which constitutes the flow of our finite experience, although it is already implicit in that experience and may, under the proper conditions, be contained in and transform it. For all consciousness is the manifestation in us of the mind of God, with some degree of adequacy: and however small that degree may be, all consciousness is self-reflective and self-transcendent. All ideas are modes in the attribute of thought, and that is one of the infinite ways in which God's essence is expressed.

So Spinoza says "we feel ourselves to be eternal." In our self-awareness and reflective consciousness this is indeed the case; and in the ultimate achievement of intuitive knowledge, the intellectual love of God, the human mind becomes identified with at least some part of the divine intellect and so is eternal and deathless; in a significant sense, it is immortal.

Immortality is, however, an ambiguous term, and Spinoza's conception of it may be, and often is, altogether misunderstood. As commonly used the word means an extension of our conscious life through an indefinite—in fact, unending—time. Such a notion for Spinoza would be sheer confusion. Time is the form of existence peculiar to the finite, which comes to be and passes away within finite limits. The order of time is the appropriate form of the imaginative consciousness, but is not the order of the intellect. The latter is the eternal order (the logical order), complete and self-contained, in which there is no flux and no succession—for "in eternity there is no *when, before* or *after*." Whatever participates in the order of time comes to an end, passes away, is finite and mortal, and only the infinite and eternal, what transcends the order of time altogether, is properly called immortal.

For Spinoza, therefore, immortality is not an indefinitely extended after-life in which the mind persists through time after the death of the body. The idea of the body, so far as that is the temporal stream of consciousness, in sense-perception, imagination, and memory, is identical with the body in substance. As a finite mode of extension the body necessarily comes to an end in time and is destroyed. The mind, the idea of the body, as a finite mode of thought, is dissipated in consequence when the body ceases to maintain itself. But no idea is *merely* finite, no idea is simply a temporal event in the conscious stream of human experience, although every idea we entertain is at least that. It is also self-reflective; there is at the same time an idea of the idea. Through this self-reflective capacity, the human mind can conceive the eternal, by converting imaginative, sensuous, ideas into adequate thinking, which grasps its objects *sub specie aeternitatis* and comprehends time as an order, complete and whole, in its entirety. Hegel, writing two centuries after Spinoza, remarks that time itself, in its concept, is eternal. Spinoza understood this (and Hegel may well have had him in mind). The temporal order raised to the level of intellect and understood in the comprehension of reason as the self-manifestation of the nature (or essence) of God, is eternity, for the intellect, purged of imaginal confusion, transcends the flux of time.

This is why the knowledge of God through *scientia intuitiva*, the comprehension of the whole in a single act of intuition, is eternal and deathless, and the human mind is not exhausted by the stream of *imaginatio*. As Spinoza puts it in a much misunderstood proposition:

> The human mind cannot be absolutely destroyed with the body, but there is something of it besides (*ejus aliquid remanet*) which is eternal. (*Ethics*, V, xxiii)

It is not that something "remains," persists, or survives in time after the death of the body, but something that is not accounted for as mere imaginative and fleeting experience, which remains to be considered—something that is eternal and that transcends the stream of temporal occurrence altogether.

Such transcendent awareness is adequate knowledge. While it is a knowledge of the infinite self-determinacy of Substance, it is also in one way still an idea of the body, for the body is not, any more than the mind, simply finite and restricted to the confined limits of its apparent spatio-temporal dimensions. The body is an organic activity in dynamic relations with the whole physical universe, so that the whole physical universe is in some way or other reflected in it. The principle of structure, which maintains the "face of the whole universe" as one invariant individual whole, is immanent in every part, in every body, and is, in a complex organism such as the human frame, registered in greater detail and is more distinctly mirrored. The idea of the body, reflectively raised, so to speak, to its highest power, is thus the adequate consciousness of the principle of the whole, the eternal order that comprehends time as such, as well as space as a complete totality. All this is implicit in the nature of the body itself and becomes explicit in its idea. Similarly, each body is implied and determinately involved in the nature of Substance, so the adequate idea of the human body (what we are here concerned with), its idea *sub specie aeternitatis*, is eternally in the intellect of God. And this adequate idea is, likewise, the adequate idea of the human mind, which is identical with its reflective awareness, and in its adequate conception is identical with the intellect of God. It is the eternal idea of the eternal, of which the transient and mortal stream of consciousness is but the inadequate temporal manifestation.

Such is the immortality of the human soul. It is the adequate knowledge in which the mind is one with the mind of God, and in the light of which conduct is free and virtuous, entirely satisfying and emotionally as well as morally and intellectually adequate. It is the realization of wholeness in the finite person—the self-fulfilment of the infinite in its finite manifestation, which is possible only at the level of reflective consciousness. In the over-arching comprehension of the nature of God and the universe, in the understanding of the place of the finite within the entire system, the importance of the body as a finite mode and the temporary effects upon it of external causes shrink to virtual insignificance, and temporal events lose their hold upon us and their emotional effects decline in force. We are then no longer deeply concerned about the transient matters and are not disconcerted by "the slings and arrows of outrageous fortune." In the Scholium to the 39th proposition of Part V of the *Ethics* Spinoza writes:

> So far as human bodies are capable of many [acts], there is no doubt that their natures can be referred to minds which have a great awareness of themselves and of God, and of which the greater part and the most important is eternal, and that therefore they should scarcely fear death.

For such minds the brevity of human life is merely incidental, for their consciousness embraces all time and all existence in an eternal concept of the whole.

Free action and virtuous conduct, we have seen, is its own reward, just as passion and vice is in itself misery and frustration. True blessedness is the knowledge and intellectual love of God, beyond which nothing further is needed or desirable. To contemplate an "afterlife," therefore, in which human beings are rewarded for virtue with carnal pleasures, or punished for their sins in eternal torment is utterly absurd. Human immortality is something very different and much more admirable and desirable.

Spinoza's conclusion to his greatest work makes a fitting ending to this brief exposition of his philosophy and may, in conclusion, be quoted in full:

> I have resolved all the things which I wished to demonstrate about the power of the mind over the affects and the mind's freedom; from which it is apparent how much the wise man prevails over, and is more capable than, the ignorant, who is moved only by lust. For an ignorant person, besides being agitated in many ways by external causes, and enjoying no true contentment of mind, lives as if unaware of himself, of God and of reality, and as soon as he ceases to suffer, ceases to be. The wise, in contrast, so far as considered as such, is scarcely moved in spirit, but is conscious, by a certain and eternal necessity, of self, of God and of things, never ceases to be, but always enjoys true contentment of spirit. If now the way, which I have shown leads to this, seems very difficult, yet it can be found. And indeed that must be difficult which is so seldom discovered. For how could it come about, if salvation were at hand and could be acquired without great labor, that it should be neglected by almost everybody? But all excellent things are as difficult as they are rare.

Epilogue

For PROFUNDITY, COMPREHENSIVENESS, and systematic coherence few philosophical treatises can rival Spinoza's *Ethics*. His philosophy is extraordinary for its success in reconciling opposing viewpoints and going beyond either. He agrees with the empiricists that knowledge begins with and is rooted in sense, but he differs with them by denying that sense-perception (or something external to the mind that is supposed to correspond to it) can serve as a criterion of truth. At the same time he agrees with the rationalists that sense-perception is confused and misleading and that adequate knowledge is given only by reason and comprehension of the part in the light of the whole. Here, however, he goes beyond Rationalism, refusing to countenance a formal, linear, and abstract deduction, proceeding from abstract first principles by self-evident steps to general conclusions. Reason, for Spinoza, is the activity of developing the concrete implications of a systematically structured reality, the ordering principle of which is immanent in all its parts and modes of self-manifestation. Thus his position is neither pure Rationalism nor radical Empiricism but a combination of both which advances beyond either one of them.

In ethics he recognizes the place and importance of pleasure without being a hedonist, while his insistence on reason and its dictates as the source of morality, and on self-determination as the essence of freedom, anticipate much later thinkers (such as Kant). In politics he succeeds in reconciling the absolutism of Hobbes with the radicalism of Althusius in a consistent theory which provides a rational foundation for stable government by popular consent. In so doing he is the forerunner of Rousseau and an antidote to excessive individualism. On religion he overcomes the conflict between faith and reason, establishing the claims of the latter, while retaining respect and reverence for the former, purged of the debilitating effects of superstition. Part V of the *Ethics*, despite the stark formalism of the method of its presentation, is still capable, without any sacrifice of intellectual integrity and clarity, of arousing in the reader something approaching religious emotion—a rare quality in any philosophical writing.

117

Glossary

Affect	Emotion.
Attribute	The essence of Substance (Nature or God) as conceived by the Intellect.
Essence	Essential nature: what a thing essentially is.
formal	The real nature of the actually existing thing.
objective	The nature of the thing as represented in consciousness.
Imaginatio	Sensuous consciousness, sense-perception, imagination, and imagery; the first kind of knowledge.
Mode	A modification or affection of Substance, a way in which substance is differentiated.
finite	Limited mode, one caused by another finite mode.
infinite	A specific modification of an Attribute, following immediately from the conception of the Attribute.
Ratio	Reason; mathematical deduction; the second kind of knowledge.
Scientia intuitiva	Intuitive science; an immediate grasp of the essence or nature of things in relation to the essence, or nature, of the whole to which they belong. Defined by Spinoza as knowledge that "proceeds from an adequate idea of the formal essence of certain attributes of God to an adequate knowledge of the essence of things."

Suggested Further Reading

Hallett, H. F. *Benedict de Spinoza. The Elements of his Philosophy*. London: Athlone Press, 1957.

Hampshire, S. *Spinoza*. Harmondsworth, Baltimore: Penguin Books, 1962.

Harris, E. E. *Salvation from Despair: A Reappraisal of Spinoza's Philosophy*. The Hague: Martinus Nijhoff, 1973.

McKeon, R. P. *The Philosophy of Spinoza*. New York: Longmans, Green and Co., 1928.

Roth, L. *Spinoza*. London: Allen & Unwin, 1954.

Saw, R. L. *The Vindication of Metaphysics*. London: Macmillan, 1951.

Anthologies

Freeman, E., and Mandelbaum, M., eds. *Spinoza: Essays in Interpretation*. La Salle, IL: Open Court, 1973.

Grene, M., ed. *Spinoza, A Collection of Critical Essays*. Garden City, NY: Anchor Books, 1973.

Kashap, R., ed. *Studies in Spinoza, Critical and Interpretive Essays*. Berkeley: University of California Press, 1972.

van der Bend, J. G., ed. *Spinoza on Knowing, Being and Freedom*. Assen, Netherlands: Van Gorcum, 1974.

Wilbur, J. B., ed. *Spinoza's Metaphysics: Essays in Critical Appreciation*. Assen, Netherlands: Van Gorcum, 1976.

Index

121